HONG KONG MURDERS

HONG KONG MURDERS

KATE WHITEHEAD

OXFORD
UNIVERSITY PRESS

Oxford University Press is a department of the University of Oxford.
It furthers the University's objective of excellence in research, scholarship,
and education by publishing worldwide in

Oxford New York

Athens Auckland Bangkok Bogotá Buenos Aires Calcutta
Cape Town Chennai Dar es Salaam Delhi Florence Hong Kong Istanbul
Karachi Kuala Lumpur Madrid Melbourne Mexico City Mumbai
Nairobi Paris São Paulo Shanghai Singapore Taipei Tokyo Toronto Warsaw

with associated companies in Berlin Ibadan

Oxford is a registered trade mark of Oxford University Press

First published 2001
This impression (lowest digit)
3 5 7 9 10 8 6 4

British Library Cataloguing in Publication Data
available

Library of Congress Cataloguing-in-Publication Data
available

ISBN 0-19-591488-0

Printed in Hong Kong
Published by Oxford University Press (China) Ltd
18th Floor, Warwick House East, Taikoo Place, 979 King's Road, Quarry Bay
Hong Kong

In memory of my childhood friend,
Petra Steinwehe

Acknowledgements

Peter Barnes, Derek Bere, Harry Blud, Roderic Broadhurst, Martin Cowley, Glyn Davies, Kevin Egan, Mike Fulton, Brian Gravener, Sheilah Hamilton, Brian Heard, Peter Ip Pau-fuk, Brian Ireland, Gregory Lam Kwai-bun, Herbert Lee Kee-fun, Jimmy Leung Hung-wai, Norrie MacKillop, Brian Merritt, John Norman, Trevor Oakes, Frederick Ong, Kerry Pearce, Ray Pierce, Mike Rawlinson, Pedro Redinha, Monte Richmond, Jose Rodrigues, Harold Traver, Elsie Tu, and Steve Vickers.

Special thanks to friends Jim Atkinson, Andrew Chetham, Donna Clarke, Richard Cook, Kylie Knott, Charlotte Parsons, Rose Tang, Samantha Whitehead, Paul Williams, and Cafe Gypsy.

Contents

Introduction: Death by Myriad Swords

Every murder leaves behind a corpse, and in the heat of a Hong Kong summer decomposition is fast. Detectives must work quickly and efficiently at the scene of a crime, and the first few days are crucial as they struggle to locate evidence that will pinpoint the killer. Among the telltale signs that hint at a motive are fingerprints, not just those of the killer. Cultural fingerprints also provide clues that shed light on the psyche of Hong Kong–a complex city fresh with entrepreneurial enthusiasm yet steeped in ancient values.

By revealing these cultural fingerprints, the murders show more than tales of rage, jealousy, greed, and violence: they tell a Hong Kong story. One key to deciphering these fingerprints is to use as a framework the fundamental Confucian principle that man exists in relation to others. A Westerner may be viewed as an individual, but a Chinese person tends to exist in relation to family, friends, and colleagues. From the moment of birth, children within a Chinese culture are shown their place in the world by learning their responsibilities in relation to those around them. Great importance is placed on interpersonal relationships, especially among members of the extended family.

In general it could be said that in the United States, children are encouraged to express their individuality, while in Hong Kong the needs of the individual are suppressed in favour of the group, leaving little room for the 'loner'. That is not to say they don't exist. There have been only two serial killers in Hong Kong's history, both of whom were loners. Despite living with their families, they were untouched by the enforced intimacy of their tiny flats.

For a Chinese person, the family is the centre of their universe. It can be relied on for everything, from career advice to matrimonial prospects. Trust is implicit. This explains why many Chinese businesses draw on relatives to fill key positions, especially where money is concerned. The old adage 'blood is thicker than water' is particularly true in Hong Kong, and there can be no better example than the notorious loanshark Wong Kwai-fun. The eldest of five, he drew his brothers and sister into his loanshark empire, and the success of his business was a measure of their ability to trust each other implicitly.

The flip-side of this coin is that the Chinese can sometimes seem cold and uncaring to anyone who falls outside this inner circle. In the case of the 'Tuen Mun rapist', an estimated forty people walked over the body of one of his victims, lying in a stairwell, before her murder was reported. More shocking still, all of them were her neighbours. The general feeling was that it was 'none of their business' and they 'did not want to get involved'. More recently, in 1999, a fifteen-year-old student was raped on a stairwell in her housing estate after her next-door neighbour refused to open the door to help her flee from her attacker. Again, the neighbour 'did not want to get involved'.

A key to understanding murder in Hong Kong is the issue of 'face'—the dynamics of impression management. Chinese often take great pains not to 'lose face', so much so that a person might even kill to save it. But what will be referred to as 'face killings' are not unique to the Chinese. In the United States in the early 1980s street gangs used the expression 'don't dis[respect] me', a warning that if a rival gang member insulted them they would avenge the snub. The expression 'dis' has since lost its power by being absorbed into mainstream culture, but the sentiment remains. American gangs may be more direct than Hong Kong triads, but exhibit a similar attitude. The collectivist nature of Chinese societies means that if an individual 'loses face', the shame for that misdeed falls not only on themselves but on their group. Similarly, if that person were to 'gain face', the group would benefit from the reflected glory.

'Face killings' are murders that avenge a snub. Most of the 'face blood' is spilt by the Eastern equivalent of the Mafia, known as the triads, which infiltrate every aspect of Chinese culture. The tale of an infamous triad Andley Chan, nicknamed the Tiger of Wan Chai, illustrates how a minor slight can lead to a series of tit-for-tat attacks and escalate to murder. The initial incident may well have been shrugged off in some societies, but Hong Kong triads do not treat matters as lightly, especially when face is at stake. The detective who led the team that cracked the Tiger's extortion attempt, Chief Inspector Jimmy Leung, says: 'The triads believe in an eye for an eye; it is their way of settling business.'

If a loss of face comes from within the social circle, things become more complicated. The offended party might wait years for the perfect moment to air their grievance or seek revenge. In 1998, an eighty-five-year-old man killed his best friend of seventy years over an insult made sixty years earlier. Why had he waited all those years before raising the issue? Quite simply, it had not been convenient to do so before as they shared many interests, largely through family and business. But since they had both retired and their wives passed away, the man decided it was time to avenge the grudge he had borne for all those years.

Nonetheless, gang wars aside, Hong Kong does not have the culture of violence that is endemic in many Western cities, mainly because in general the Chinese shy away from aggressive behaviour. They do not have a propensity for irrational violence and only use physical force in extreme circumstances. Gratuitous violence is almost unheard of. For example, if a couple is tied up during a robbery, the chances of the woman being raped and the man abused or killed are low. The Chinese will do anything to avoid open conflict. Dissatisfaction may be expressed in a subtle or indirect way or middle-men may be used to save face. Most Westerners may believe that open discussion is the best way of avoiding conflict, but in Hong Kong it is to be avoided at all costs.

From an early age, Chinese children are discouraged from fighting, and any kind of physical violence is frowned upon, whereas in Western societies children are often encouraged to 'stick up for themselves'. Thus in Hong Kong, self-control and emotional restraint are valued qualities. Verbal insults, however, are more acceptable, and when tempers flare the Chinese tend to hurl verbal abuse.

Data kept since the 1950s show that the instances of murder and manslaughter have increased far more slowly than other forms of violent crimes. In 1956–57, there were an average of 1.4 cases of murder or manslaughter per 100,000 people. By 1989–90, this figure has increased only slightly to 1.9. There was a sharp rise in the murder/manslaughter rate in 1967–68, but this can probably be traced back to the 1967 riots, which resulted in more than 50 deaths.

Hong Kong averages fewer than 100 murders a year, far less than other large cities. Strict gun control measures ensure that the random shootings that plague the United States are not part of the Hong Kong picture. For this reason, the weapon of choice in Hong Kong is a chopper. Every Hong Kong kitchen has one—a flat, razor-sharp blade about 25 cm long and 10 cm wide with a wooden or metal handle. Triads traditionally use a chopper in their attacks. If the victim is to be murdered, the whole body will be lacerated and left to bleed to death. This is the traditional killing known as 'death by myriad swords'. But many choppings are intended merely to teach a lesson and the cleaver will be used on the victim's arms. The result may be deep lacerations on their forearms and even a lost finger—but the victim will live.

Hong Kong is one of the most densely populated places in the world. Living in crowded conditions—often three generations under one roof—necessarily makes the Hong Kong Chinese more tolerant of physical closeness. Hong Kong's 'cage men' have the worst living conditions. The high demand for labourers in the 1950s and 1960s brought many men slipping over the border from the Mainland. They were poorly paid and most lived from day to day, without marrying. With no family for support in their old age, many resorted to the cheapest accommodation available—caged homes. These 'homes', which still exist in parts of urban Hong Kong today, consist of a six-foot bed space enclosed with wire. Doubled up like bunk beds, there may be up to 45 per dormitory. In 1991, a seventy-two-year-old 'cage man' flew into a rage over his neighbour's loud radio. He chained the front door, poured paraffin under it and threw in a match. Thirteen of the thirty-six occupants were burnt to death.

Hong Kong's over-crowding presents a unique hurdle for murderers. The 'Jars Killer' was a taxi driver, so he was able to use his cab to dump his corpses in remote areas. But a lack of private transport has driven other killers to come up with more imaginative ways of hiding their victims. The sea is one option. On occasion corpses do wash up, but the waters surrounding Hong Kong may hide many hundreds of 'missing persons' whose horrific stories will never be heard.

Dangerous Liaisons

The men in the two stories that follow both broke the rules, yet they acted in entirely different ways and for entirely different reasons. Arrogance was the only thing they had in common; perhaps that was why they thought they could get away with breaking the law. They shared little else. One stood for all things American and the other coveted colonialism.

Returning to Hong Kong from the United States, Patrick Wong discovered that his status had suddenly been elevated. Women adored his American accent and attitudes, and soon he was living the life of a playboy. John MacLennan found that in Hong Kong he was hot property, too, but in a very different way. While Wong had women falling at his feet, MacLennan preferred the company of men. Being gay was hard enough in the 1970s, but especially tough because he was a police officer.

At that time, Legislator Elsie Tu harboured a deep-seated mistrust of the local police force, which led her to become involved in MacLennan's case. Largely through her efforts the affair entered the public arena, with the result that homosexuality was openly discussed in Hong Kong for the first time. Ten years later, Elsie Tu found herself fighting under the gay banner and with her help the law changed. In 1991 homosexuality became legal. The new law did not spell an immediate change in attitudes, however, and in 1992, the first gay pride march had to be cancelled because gays were too afraid to take to the streets. But over the years, the return home of students from Western universities and an increasing appreciation of the value of the 'pink dollar' have led to more liberal attitudes.

Patrick, Brenda, and Kitty: Three's a Crowd

The pastor looked uneasily across the breakfast table at his wife. She frowned and pointed accusingly at the ceiling. He nodded. The stench was still there, even stronger than before. It caught in the back of her throat, a fishy smell, like shrimp paste. A few days had passed since they noticed the stink and with it a strange fluid in the outside drain. The fluid did not flow so much as ooze, a filthy brown sludge punctuated with putrid globules.

One of the selling points of the Spanish-style villa had been that they would have few neighbours. The pastor and his wife had lived peacefully in the ground-floor flat for five years and it was only when the Chinese-American moved in upstairs that they began to feel uncomfortable. He had rented the two upper floors for a year and although he was quiet, he was not the clean-cut family man the pastor would have liked as his neighbour. He was tall, good-looking, and enjoyed fast cars. He parked his Mercedes in the front, and would come and go at all hours, often with a woman in tow. But that was none of their business; they didn't know his name and preferred it that way. If it were not for the vile stench, years could have passed without a word being exchanged between them. Yet the pastor had a sneaking suspicion he knew what the young man was up to.

That afternoon, a woman who had been living with the upstairs neighbour for a few months knocked on the pastor's door. She had shoulder-length hair and a girlish look about her. She introduced herself as Kitty and apologized for the stink. She said her goldfish had died and the dead fish was causing the foul smell. The pastor and his wife exchanged wary looks but said nothing. A couple of hours later, the Chinese-American himself knocked on the door. He had dark bags under his eyes, but he spoke animatedly. He said his name was Patrick Wong and he apologized about the stench. Not only had the goldfish died, but the rabbits as well. The pastor felt he was being taken for a fool and lost his temper. He told Patrick he would not stand for anything illegal going on in the building; he was, after all, a man of the church. Patrick assured him everything was above board and said he had arranged for a cleaner to wash the stairs.

Half an hour later, the pastor heard voices in the stairwell and opened the door just wide enough to glimpse a young Filipina, presumably the cleaner, on her hands and knees scrubbing the floor. He quickly shut the door. The smell on the stairs between the ground floor and first floor was bad, but it was even worse between the second and top floors. One hour and a bucket of disinfectant later and the vile smell remained.

The pastor's wife spent the next morning lighting incense and spraying air-freshener, but she could not mask the stench. At her wit's end, she telephoned her husband and told him he would have to call the police. The pastor's call was put through to Kerry Pearce, a hard-working, hard-drinking Australian detective. Pearce listened to the pastor's complaint half-heartedly; he had more important things to do than deal with the petty squabbles of neighbours. But he began scribbling notes when the pastor confided his suspicions. The clergyman suspected the stink could mean only one thing: his neighbour was making drugs. Pearce took down the address and said he would deal with the matter.

An officer rang Patrick's doorbell early in the morning and when no one answered, he and three other officers broke down the door. Two of the men ran upstairs and the other two searched the first floor. Patrick was in the bathroom, toothbrush in his mouth, and he did his best to look surprised, though he must have heard the police breaking the door down. The police frisked him and demanded to know where the drugs were. Patrick took them into the living room and walked over to the coffee table. It was cluttered with magazines, videos, and drug paraphernalia. A small plastic bag of cocaine lay next to an abandoned line on a smudged mirror; it looked as though Patrick had been partying when they arrived. The policemen shook him, demanding to know where the rest of the drugs were, but Patrick insisted that was all he had. One of the officers sifted through the chaos on the table. A letter caught his attention, but it was postmarked five months earlier and he cast it aside. It would be scrutinized later, as would an inscription on the back of the envelope. The words, in Patrick's handwriting, were those of a desperate man: 'This thing upon me, like a flower and a feast. This thing upon me, crawling like a snake. It is not death, but dying will solve its power'.

Patrick was taken upstairs. The second-floor living room stood empty except for some bottles and boxes stacked in the corner. Despite the windows being open, the room was filled with an eerie fog and a nauseating smell, not the sweet, chemical smell of drug-making, but of something far more disturbing, more human. It was the smell of death. Kitty stood in the middle of the room looking dishevelled and slightly manic. The vile vapours emanated from the bathroom and tentacles of fog licked the side of the door. One of the officers gagged, pulled out a packet of Marlboros, and offered them around. Using the cigarettes to help mask the smell, two of the men went into the bathroom, taking Patrick with them.

A large aluminium trunk stood upended in the bath, with vapours pouring from a hole in the trunk's top. The officers demanded to know what was in the box, their voices muffled because their hands were clamped over their mouths. Patrick, grinding his teeth, looked bewildered, and when he spoke his voice was shaky. His rabbits were in the box, he said, as well as his dog, which had also died. One of the officer's pushed him aside and steadied the trunk. He grabbed a screwdriver from the window ledge and used it to prise open the box. Released from the makeshift coffin, the foul fumes struck him full in the face. He gagged and turned away. The trunk was filled with a watery sludge, and upon steadying himself, he used the screwdriver to stir the murky darkness. He felt something hard and hooked it with the screwdriver. He heard someone retch as he drew it to the surface: it was a human skull. The eyes were dark cavities and traces of flesh hung from the mouth. The rest of the body was to be dredged out of the trunk later, the limbs wrapped in cling film. A murder investigation had begun.

The cocaine, not the body, was the express reason for Patrick and Kitty's arrest. The police conducted the formalities in the living room. On closer inspection, they saw that the bottles and boxes in the corner contained bleach, acid, and caustic soda. There were also packets of scouring pads and discarded bottles of air-freshener. After receiving the obligatory caution, the suspects were asked to sign one of the officer's notebooks. Kitty wrote her name but Patrick refused. Like many Chinese brought up in the United States, he was fluent in Cantonese but could not read or write Chinese. Only after the notes were rewritten in English did Patrick put his name to them. He then asked for legal counsel.

Patrick saw a doctor before he saw a lawyer. He had been bingeing on cocaine for days and although his body ached for sleep, he was so strung out he could not sit still. Cocaine abuse also landed Kitty in hospital. The doctor insisted she have a couple of days to recuperate before police questioning. She was formally charged with drug possession while still in her sick bed and immediately snapped back, blaming Patrick for the drugs.

Patrick Wong started taking drugs after his mother died of cancer in 1987. She was a carpet designer in Hong Kong and when he learned of her illness, Patrick left his job as a New Jersey truck driver to be with her. She died a few years later and Patrick returned to America. It was then that a friend introduced him to heroin. Patrick was no angel, but he had never experimented with drugs, not even marijuana. He used heroin for several months and then switched to cocaine, preferring the euphoric confidence that the white powder gave him. His father died a few months after his mother and the death of both parents put Patrick in the money. As the eldest of four, he inherited HK$400,000 (US$51,000) and when he returned to Hong Kong permanently in 1987 he sold his mother's flat and got another HK$1 million. Patrick's life did an about-turn. As a trucker in the United States he had commanded little respect. He was poorly paid and although a womanizer, he lacked the money to really play the scene. But things were different in Hong Kong, where an American accent gave him status and where for the first time he could afford to live the indulgent lifestyle he had long coveted. He bought a fancy car and became a creature of the night. He liked nothing better than to drive to the beaches on the south side of Hong Kong Island in the early hours of the morning, tapping out lines of cocaine on the dashboard. He also became a gambler, which was how he met Kitty.

She was unhappily married and working as a cashier at the racetrack for a meagre salary. One evening Patrick collected HK$230,000 winnings and, flush with success, threw a HK$1,000 note back at Kitty. She was impressed. They exchanged phone numbers and a couple of weeks later went out for dinner. They soon became lovers, and when Kitty's marriage broke down she moved in with Patrick.

The same whim that motivated him to toss HK$1,000 at Kitty was to cost him his inheritance. Patrick was extravagant—he even carpeted his bathroom—and between the horses and his cocaine habit, what had once been a fortune soon evaporated. More sinister things then followed.

The body in the trunk had decomposed beyond recognition. The pathologist said it had been a woman in her late twenties, but he could say little more. If not for the woman's family, the body would never have been identified. A man called the police and said he was worried the victim was his niece, Brenda. When her parents had seen Patrick's building on the front page of the newspaper, they recognized it as the same villa in a photograph of their daughter and her new boyfriend. Brenda's boyfriend was surnamed Wong, and so was Patrick.

Detective Pearce met Brenda's parents that afternoon. Brenda had left home two years earlier and her landlady showed the police into her tiny room. Pearce was bowled over by what he saw. The room was stacked from floor to ceiling with beauty products. Here were powders, eyeliners, lipsticks, rouges, shampoos, moisturizers, and bottles of hairspray, all still in their cellophane wrappers. These were the perks of her job; in her line of work looks mattered and her bosses knew it. She had been an airline hostess for ten years and when her employers dispensed free beauty products to keep their girls looking good, she hoarded them.

As the police searched the room, Brenda's mother sat on the edge of the bed sobbing. Blinking through her tears, she stared at a photo of Brenda and Patrick posing in front of the Mercedes. Even though she had never met Patrick, she disliked him; his designer clothes and Mercedes smacked of the playboy. But she had said nothing to Brenda. Her only daughter had had few boyfriends and only one had been introduced to the family. Like most young Chinese women, Brenda did not discuss the men in her life with her parents. Her mother may have had no idea how or when she had met Patrick, but her aunt did. Brenda had told the aunt how Patrick's sister, also an airline hostess, introduced them in 1985. They ran into each other again three years later; Brenda was wearing her Cathay Pacific Airways uniform and Patrick recognized her immediately. Their first date was to the races. They became lovers after a few months and Brenda delighted in showing him off to her friends. His American background made him a better class of boyfriend; this was no run-of-the-mill Hong Kong guy. His accent carried the sound of success and held out the promise of a life overseas. She fell as much in love with the idea of Patrick as with the man himself. She knew about his cocaine habit, but she would help him get over that. This was the man she wanted to marry.

Brenda had not told her aunt about the cocaine, nor about the money he had borrowed. She was careful with her savings and during her ten years with Cathay had salted away HK$480,000. Although thrifty, she could be generous with people she cared about. She would always bring presents back for her family from her trips abroad and felt close enough to Patrick to lend him HK$50,000. It was not long after she had lent him the money that things began to go wrong. He did not answer her calls and although they would often not see each other for a week, he didn't seem eager for sex. One night, after Patrick had not answered her paging messages, she waited for him outside his flat. When she saw him come home with another woman, her world fell apart.

The next day she flew to London and wrote to him on hotel stationery, the letter that was found at Patrick's house. Her letter was filled with the jealousy and anguish of a jilted lover: 'I've done a lot for you that I've never done for anyone else. You still reckon that I don't know how to look after you? I know now I've never been important to you. It's nice to know that someone is looking after you, making you happy. I'd never share my boyfriend with another woman.' Kitty was not the only bone of contention: 'Don't yell at me that I don't respect you because you don't have money. You're the one who doesn't respect me because I'm not able to help you financially while she's living with you.' She mentioned money again at the end of letter: 'I hope the termination of our relationship won't turn us into enemies. After all, we did have a nice beginning. Don't worry, I won't be pressing you to return what you owe me. If you've planned not to return it, there's nothing I can do.'

The police spent over an hour in Brenda's room, sifting through her letters and bank statements. Pearce interviewed the landlady and her daughter while Brenda's fingerprints were being lifted from the bedroom door. The pathologist later confirmed that the body was Brenda's. It had been placed in the trunk in the foetal position, the left hand pressed against the side, thus escaping the corrosive effects of the acid. The pathologist was able to take the prints from the hand in the trunk and match them with Brenda's. Dental records confirmed the match as well. It was impossible to be certain how she had died as her body was so badly decomposed, but all the evidence pointed to a strong blow to the head. There was a gaping hole—13 x 5 cm—just above her left ear. The pathologist noted it would have taken more than one blow to make such an injury. He thought she must have been killed between one and four weeks earlier.

The police interrogated Patrick about the body, but he remained cool and refused to say anything. It was Kitty who stumbled into complicity. 'I've got nothing to do with the body. It was Patrick who did it,' she blurted out. Pearce could not believe his luck. If she had kept quiet, like Patrick, he would have struggled to find something concrete with which to charge them, but her accusation gave him something to work on and he pushed her to tell her story.

Kitty said she had been at Patrick's house that night and in the morning played poker with him and Brenda. When they had finished the game, Patrick went into the bedroom with Brenda, while Kitty remained in the living room taking cocaine and watching television. She watched cartoons for a while and when the horse racing came on, she knocked on Patrick's bedroom door and asked if he was going to place any bets. His room was messy and although Patrick was up, Brenda was still in bed. When Brenda did not answer her, she shook her but she did not move. Kitty said she wanted to call an ambulance, but Patrick threatened to beat her if she did. When she tried to leave, Patrick blocked her way, warning that if she left he would blame her.

Pearce took down Kitty's statement and sent it to be typed up. However, when he sent someone to pick up the report, it had gone missing. Pearce was furious. He quizzed the typists and opened an internal investigation, but the probe turned up nothing. When he found out more about Kitty's background, however, his suspicions that the report had been removed were confirmed. Both Kitty's father and sister were police officers.

Within a week, Pearce had a clearer picture of the events. On the night that Brenda disappeared, the landlady's daughter was unable to sleep. She was lying awake in bed at 5am when she heard Brenda go to the toilet. Five minutes later, she heard the phone ring and Brenda rush to answer it. One of Patrick's neighbours heard her an hour later; he had been woken by the sound of women quarrelling. As the row escalated, they swore at each other, their curses becoming increasingly obscene. It sounded as if violence would be used and then he heard a man's voice intervene. He said it sounded as though the man was taking the side of one of the women, that the other felt bullied, and then there was silence.

Brenda was rostered to fly to Frankfurt the next day. The flight was scheduled to leave at 10.40pm and cabin crew usually report for duty an hour before take-off. At 6pm, Cathay Crew Control received a call from a woman claiming to be Brenda Wong who said that she was ill and had been given four days' sick leave. There was nothing unusual about this; it is standard procedure as long as the call is followed up by a doctor's certificate. But no doctor's note followed.

Meanwhile, Brenda's credit cards were being run up to the hilt. The day after she went missing, close to HK$40,000 was rung up on her Visa card and Gold card. The forged signature was eventually traced back to Kitty. It was not her first such offence; she was already under investigation for exploring the upper limits of her unwitting boss's credit card. This time Kitty went on a manic spending spree. Alternating between the two cards, she bought gold necklaces and bracelets from four jewellery shops. Then she called a hotel florist and ordered half a dozen pink roses. She said they were for her sister, gave Brenda's address, and paid for them with the Visa card. When Brenda's landlady saw the flowers on the doorstep, she thought they were from her boyfriend and took them inside. It wasn't until she read the attached note—'Betty Wong, Happy Birthday, from Brenda'—that she realized her mistake, tucked the card under Brenda's door, and left the flowers outside.

The flowers were not Kitty's last purchase that day. She went to a hardware shop and stocked up on the things one might need to try to dissolve a body: eight bottles of caustic soda, eight bottles of nitric acid, and alcohol. Even this was not enough and two days later she was back for more. Pearce collected the receipts for the chemicals, as well as the aluminium trunk, and testimonies from the shopkeepers. There were statements from colleagues, neighbours, friends, and family. The evidence was considerable, but was it enough for a murder conviction? To most people, the known facts of the case might seem quite damning evidence of murder, but in a court of law things are less straightforward. There was nothing linking Patrick and Kitty to the moment of death, such as bloody fingerprints on a murder weapon. They could certainly be convicted of preventing a proper burial, but the police believed they were guilty of more than that and they were determined to prove it.

One of Hong Kong's most controversial and charismatic barristers, Kevin Egan, was up for the case. Pearce and Egan had a grudging respect for each other. They had little in common, aside from both being

Australians who enjoyed their drink, but they had a good working relationship. Pearce gave Egan a rundown of the events and took him through the evidence. He showed him photos from the scene, receipts, reports, statements, and Brenda's letter. Tossing the envelope on the table, he asked Egan if he could make anything of the bizarre inscription. Egan read it aloud: 'This thing upon me, like a flower and a feast. This thing upon me, crawling like a snake. It is not death, but dying will solve its power.' The barrister was unusually quiet and then he gave a full belly laugh. He recognized the words from the film *Barfly*, and he filled Pearce in on the movie based on the writer Charles Bukowsky. Egan was ready to take on the case. He grinned at Pearce and shot him one of his favourite lines: 'When you haven't got enough evidence, you've got to come out with all guns blazing.' The defence complained there was not enough evidence for a conviction, but words were whispered in judicial ears and the case went ahead. Eager to make sure the jury were familiar with *Barfly*, Egan arranged for a special screening in court. The jury watched the film in awe, some studiously taking notes. The rest of the whisky-driven lyricism that Patrick had jotted down read: 'As I drop this last desperate pen in some cheap motel, they will find me here. And no one will know my name, my meaning, nor the treasure of my escape.'

The words must have had a special meaning for Patrick, but he was giving nothing away. From the minute he asked for a lawyer, he had remained silent. It was Kitty who did all the talking. They had been separated since their arrest, but before their trial they were allowed to see each other briefly. Eager to find out how closely involved they were, the police took advantage of a special court privilege, which allowed them to eavesdrop on the suspects' private conversation. One of Pearce's men sat in the adjoining room monitoring their conversation. Five minutes into the meeting, Pearce asked what they were talking about. The listener grimaced, shrugged his shoulders, and offered Pearce the earpiece. He could hear no words being exchanged, just a slow sucking sound. Pearce laughed and told the officer he thought Kitty and Patrick still seemed to be getting on very well; she was performing oral sex on him.

The court case lasted fifteen days. In mid-August 1990, the jury returned a guilty verdict and both Patrick and Kitty were sentenced to death, which in Hong Kong in fact means life imprisonment. Patrick jumped to his feet and spoke out for the first time, pleading with the judge: 'I did not do it, sir.' But the judge was not about to be swayed and he condemned Patrick for his 'evil and utterly revolting' crime. Pearce was satisfied with the result; this was the first time in Hong Kong two people had been sentenced on circumstantial evidence. He knew they would try to appeal, so he made sure they had an extra five years added to their sentences for preventing a proper burial.

Locked in his cell for twenty-two hours a day, Patrick spent much of the time reading. Visiting hours were limited, but he was not short of company. Even behind bars he still managed to act as a magnet for women. A young British woman who worked as an escort would bring him books and Kitty's sister, Grace, supplied him with toiletries. Patrick might have been in jail, but he still wanted to make sure he looked good. He even had her buy him a HK$4,000 pair of shoes. Grace brought him more than deodorant; she also acted as a go-between. After nearly a year in jail, Patrick told Grace to tell her sister that she should write to the United States consulate about the 'old story'. He said her letter would help his defence and as soon as he was freed he would ask for compensation and use that money for Kitty's defence. Kitty did as Patrick asked and Grace took the letter to the consulate.

Prison did not curb Patrick's appetite for women. He noticed Shirley Wong, a volunteer visitor, when she was seeing a fellow inmate and determined that she should visit him as well. He asked the prisoner if he would mind if she saw him, too, and so Shirley became one of his regular visitors.

It was easy to see why Patrick liked her. She was young, beautiful, and idealistic. She had gone to a Christian school and was a member of the Children of God religious sect. Patrick turned on the charm and Shirley began to fall for the suave prisoner. Her job as a freelance beautician gave her the time to travel to Stanley Prison, on the south side of Hong Kong Island, from her home in Kowloon. A sheet of glass separated them during their meetings and they talked to each other on the prison phone. Shirley introduced Patrick to God and he quickly adopted her faith. The prison priest showed him scriptures, which he would spend hours studying each day, and he eventually received Holy Communion. Patrick proposed to Shirley in prison and she accepted. Few people attended their small prison wedding, not even Shirley's parents. She was afraid her parents would disapprove and had not even told them she visited inmates.

Patrick kept his wedding a secret from Kitty because he did not want her to back down from her agreement to push for a retrial. Kitty had said she would tell her lawyers that she wanted to tell the truth about events. It was the nature of their lies that formed the legal grounds for an appeal. The judge had said during the trial that the jury should consider lies as evidence to prove guilt. But the prosecutor countered that although lies could ruin a defendant's credibility, they were not enough to prove guilt.

Patrick and Kitty were back in the High Court in March 1993. They had not seen each other in two and a half years, and Patrick now told her that he had married. The colour drained from Kitty's face; she felt angry, then humiliated, and looked down at the ground and said nothing.

The retrial was based on Kitty's affidavit in which she absolved Patrick of all blame. She said she and Brenda had argued over Patrick and that Brenda had hit her with a hammer. Kitty claimed she hit her back in self-defence, and although she admitted trying to get rid Brenda's body, she denied she was guilty of murder. Yet many questions remained unanswered, the prime one being what Patrick had thought was causing the vile stench. He insisted cocaine abuse had killed his sense of smell and, to prove his point, he stood up in court and pulled a tissue through a hole in the side of his nose. Cocaine, he said, had worn away his nasal membrane. Patrick's reason for blaming the stink on a couple of dead rabbits was even more bizarre. He said he had lied to protect his dog, which had been defecating in the flat.

Patrick complained that all his troubles were a result of women and he showed no kindness to Kitty. He denied that their relationship was one of master and slave, insisting that she was the domineering one. He berated her for making him lose HK$800,000 by giving him bad tips when she was working at the racetrack. He cast Brenda as the heroine and said he had loved her and had intended to marry her. He insisted he did not owe her money; the comment in her letter 'I won't be pressing you to return what you owe' was a reference to affection and not to the HK$50,000 she had lent him.

Patrick's lawyer told the jury he knew Patrick was a womanizer and a cocaine abuser, but that he was not on trial for his morals. Desperate to have her husband freed, Shirley rushed from the gallery and threw herself on her knees in front of the jury. She insisted Patrick was innocent and pleaded with the jury: 'I'm a Christian; I don't tell lies. If I did I would be struck down dead on the street.' The jury appeared to be moved, but the judge took a less kindly view of the outburst and banned her from the court.

Patrick clutched a little red Bible to his chest throughout the trial and was still clasping it when the verdict of 'not guilty' was announced. It seemed to take him minutes to realize he was free, and then he ran outside where Shirley showered him with kisses. The judge did not hide his amazement at the verdict and said to Kitty: 'It would appear, however surprising it may be, that the jury have accepted what you gave in your affirmation.' Kitty was given seven years for manslaughter. Both she and Patrick were given the additional five years for preventing a proper burial. Patrick disputed the charge and, spotting the man who had prosecuted him so ably, strode over to Kevin Egan and asked him if he would be willing to switch roles and defend him this time. Egan was taken aback. Patrick, he said later, was totally amoral, a man who saw no right or wrong, only opportunities. Patrick went to court over the charge, won the case and was free.

It was not long before another opportunity came Patrick's way. A controversial entrepreneur decided to cash in on the sensational case and asked Patrick to star in a telephone hotline called 'Melted Carcass'. Callers were charged HK$10 per minute and could choose from seven topics recorded not only by Patrick, but by his wife Shirley as well. Patrick expounded on the nature of love, sex, and relationships and came out with such philosophical points as: 'Love and sex are two different things. I could not differentiate this before. I liked many people. But as I grow older, I know what love is.' Within a week, Patrick had made HK$1 million from the hotline. But as for his new-found awareness of relationships, he was not as successful. Eighteen months after he was freed, Patrick and Shirley separated.

2

John MacLennan: Skeleton in Hong Kong's Closet

John MacLennan had five bullet holes in his chest when he was found sprawled on his bedroom floor on 15 January 1980. Like the man himself, his death was not quiet. Many talked about MacLennan, but few really knew him and it took a year-long investigation to piece together what had happened.

John MacLennan was born into a simple farming family in Ross-shire, Scotland. His parents were down-to-earth country folk and when his elder brother began to work the land, it was assumed John would follow. But he wanted more from life and the police seemed to offer everything he had dreamed of; he coveted the uniform, the pomp and ceremony, and the respect that the job commanded. It was with his parents' blessing that he joined the local force. Within four years MacLennan rose from cadet to constable, but he still hungered for excitement and when he heard of jobs with the Royal Hong Kong Police, he applied. A couple of months later, he found himself on the other side of the world.

MacLennan got off to a shaky start in Hong Kong. After his obligatory six months at the training school, he was criticized for his stubbornness, tendency to draw attention to himself, and poor handling of weapons. But he proved himself in his first posting with an emergency unit and his second, a year later, saw an equally favourable report from his boss in the Criminal Investigation Department.

MacLennan took to Hong Kong quickly; the city gave him the freedom to be the man he had always wanted to be. He missed his family, especially his mother, whom he wrote to weekly, but away from his parents' frugal existence he revelled in playing the colonial. Winston Churchill was his hero and he was devoted to the royal family, but his greatest pride was being a police officer and he was loud in condemnation of anyone who brought shame on the force. MacLennan was a stickler for punctuality and was always well presented in a jacket and tie. If casual wear was called for, he wore a safari suit; jeans were not his style. Formal occasions meant a kilt, and when he got home drunk and homesick in the early hours he would often listen to the bagpipes at full volume.

MacLennan enjoyed his drink, but he was not always pleasant company when drunk. Alcohol could make him arrogant, and for all those who enjoyed his company, there were just as many who found him tediously self-obsessed. Partly for this reason, he found himself with more acquaintances than close friends. His best friend was Christopher Burns, another Scottish policeman who had joined the force at the same time as MacLennan. During their first couple of years in Hong Kong, before Burns married, they spent a lot of their free time together exploring the city's more dubious nightlife. They trawled the 'girlie bars' and low-end nightclubs and MacLennan would sometimes bring home a prostitute. Burns considered his friend a womanizer, but he couldn't have been more wrong. MacLennan could be charming to women, and he enjoyed playing the gentleman and flirting, but it was men that MacLennan was interested in, Chinese men in particular. He stumbled upon Hong Kong's underground gay scene and was soon seeing a couple of Chinese boys regularly, arranged by a triad pimp called Molo Tsui. He especially liked an eighteen-year-old boy, Ah Tung, and wanted him to move in with him, but the teenager was reluctant.

MacLennan's lifestyle was expensive; between the boys and the drink he had always spent all of his salary by the end of each month. For someone with a conservative outlook, he was lackadaisical about his financial affairs, but scrupulous about his private ones. He managed to fool most of his friends. If they had discovered his secret it would have shattered the pompous image he had so carefully cultivated. It would also have been a crime.

Britain decriminalized homosexuality in 1967 but Hong Kong clung onto the antiquated law. The city has long been a hiding place for lost souls seeking to break free of their past and reinvent themselves, and in the 1970s there was a considerable number of gay Western men in both the police and the government. Hong Kong's gay community was one of the concerns of Special Branch. This low-profile department kept tabs on homosexuals within the force and government. Special Branch's records, as much rumour and hearsay as fact, had been kept since 1966.

A tour of duty lasted two and a half years and when MacLennan's contract ended he went home on leave. Before he left, his boss praised his work and recommended a pay rise. MacLennan had asked to work in Special Branch and while he was on holiday his request was granted. In March 1977, he began his new post in Special Branch's vetting section. There he had access to files listing the names of suspected homosexuals and details of their liaisons. There were many civil servants rumoured to be gay, among them the Police Commissioner, Roy Henry. MacLennan would later describe what he had seen at Special Branch as 'political dynamite that would blow the lid off the colony'. The files must have made MacLennan nervous, for soon after joining the department he decided he wanted out and applied to the Metropolitan Police in London. His resignation after just two months was a shock to the head of Special Branch, who was angry MacLennan had not even hinted about leaving. He transferred the inspector to another post, away from the 'black book' of homosexuals, to serve out his notice.

Routine police work in London did not live up to MacLennan's expectations and he pined for the Hong Kong lifestyle. In March 1978, just nine months after he had left, MacLennan was back for another tour of duty. This time he was stationed as a police inspector in Yuen Long, a town in the north-west New Territories. It was no accident that he was posted to such a quiet backwater; officers who failed to endear themselves to their superiors invariably found themselves in the more remote districts. But MacLennan did not mind. He was happy in Yuen Long and at weekends would go to the bars in Tsim Sha Tsui. One of his favourite watering holes was the Waltzing Matilda Inn, a lively bar that was also a popular gay haunt. MacLennan was always discreet about his affairs and would ignore his Chinese lovers if British friends were around. With an audience and a few drinks in him, he could become racist towards the Chinese. But when he was alone, he would chat up the young waiters.

Four months into his new posting, in the summer of 1978, MacLennan ran into an ex-policeman, Ah Keung, who wanted to introduce him to his friend. 'You're both from Scotland,' Ah Keung said as he introduced him to David Lau, who was studying in Glasgow but spending the summer with his grandmother. Lau was seventeen years old and toying with the idea of joining the police. Ah Keung hoped MacLennan might tell him how to go about it and gave him the student's telephone number.

A couple of days later, MacLennan called Lau and offered to buy him lunch. Over the meal he explained the qualifications he would need to join the police and suggested they get an application form from his office. They took a taxi to the station, but instead of going to MacLennan's office, they went to his flat; he said the papers were there. MacLennan turned the television on and they watched cartoons in silence. Afraid of appearing too pushy, Lau did not mention the forms. MacLennan took a shower, then came out of the bathroom with a towel wrapped around his waist and suggested Lau shower as well. The teenager declined, but MacLennan persisted, saying it was such a hot day. When Lau was getting dressed in the bedroom, MacLennan coaxed him onto the bed. 'I love Chinese flesh,' he murmured and ran his hands over Lau. 'It's all right, I'm not going to make love to you, I just want to borrow your hands.' Lau pushed him away, repulsed by the advances, but when he got to the front door he felt sorry for him. 'It's okay, I know about these things,' Lau said, closing the door behind him as he left.

MacLennan called the student a few days later to apologize. The inspector was embarrassed and hoped he hadn't upset him. Lau told him not to worry. The matter would have been left at that, an awkward pass, had the student not told a friend. Lau's friend thought the story amusing and told his father, a former police sergeant, who took the matter seriously. He suggested Lau make a report and although the student was initially reluctant, he decided it was the best thing to do in case MacLennan tried such things with another boy. The allegation was investigated internally. It took six weeks to conclude that there was a 'ring of truth' to the complaint and the report was passed to a handful of senior officers. The general opinion was that since the student had returned to Scotland, MacLennan should be given a verbal warning and the matter dropped. That would have been the case if the New Territories' District Commander hadn't made his view known. He had met MacLennan only once in the officer's mess. The inspector had had a few drinks and was holding court in his rather arrogant manner. The commander took an instant dislike to him. He was sure MacLennan was gay and made that clear in his memo: 'I would not wish him [MacLennan] to remain in this district...We have adequate knowledge but surely no prolonged or exhaustive study of this man is going to alter what he clearly is and will continue to be [homosexual].' On the strength of the commander's disgust, it was decided MacLennan should be dismissed; he would be given a month's salary in lieu of notice and passage home.

Homosexuality was a hot topic. In August 1978, a prominent solicitor, Richard Duffy, had been jailed for having sex with underage boys. Police raids on his luxurious flat had turned up boxes of photos of boys as young as ten years old in bondage, and the bunk beds in the flat suggested that he had more than one young Chinese lover living with him. The case brought up lots of information about the homosexual scene and revealed that it was far more organized than police had suspected. Hoping to shorten his sentence, Duffy agreed to talk about the gay prostitution rings and the triads who ran them. The information overwhelmed Special Branch and a department was set up to deal with Duffy's leads. Officially called the Special Investigations Unit (SIU), the unit was headed by Superintendent Brooks. Tall and slim, Brooks acted the macho cop. His drinking buddy and second in command was Chief Inspector Mick Quinn, a portly officer with a ruddy drinker's complexion. Half a dozen other men made up the team. Brooks and Quinn were not the most charming of officers. As children they had probably been bullies; in the police they were just doing their jobs. They were naturally homophobic and given the law, they were self-righteous in their condemnation of the men they were to investigate. But they chose their targets carefully. Limited resources meant they had to prioritize cases. If they took a dislike to someone, they could make his life miserable.

Duffy was keen to get out of jail and he talked freely. One of the triads he named was Molo Tsui, the same pimp who had arranged some of MacLennan's liaisons. Molo Tsui would lurk in the shadows of Hong Kong's first gay club, Disco Disco, looking for young boys who were new to the scene. He would recruit the youngsters for civil servants who were reluctant to risk being seen in well-known gay hangouts and were willing to pay a go-between. He had the names of many prominent people on his books, from senior government official and heads of banks to police officers. The SIU was well aware of the potential blackmail risk Molo Tsui posed, and he was eventually jailed. One of the names Duffy mentioned was Mike Fulton, another police officer. Duffy had defended a number of triads that Fulton had arrested and knew that Fulton was gay. Since Duffy had never liked the officer, he suggested that Fulton would make a good informant. Brooks and Quinn weren't bothered about arresting Fulton; they merely intended to use him to target other homosexuals.

When MacLennan was told of his dismissal, his world collapsed. He immediately protested his innocence and insisted the complaint must have come from a triad. Terrified of being expelled from the force, he called on everyone he thought might be able to help. He turned to his former boss and, in the same breath that he told of his dismissal, he mentioned the files he had seen at Special Branch. He did not mention any names, saying it was more than his life was worth to discuss it. He had a solicitor draft a petition on his behalf to the governor and then went to a magistrate with his story. If Lau's allegation was the only reason for his dismissal, he said he at least deserved the opportunity to have his say in court. The magistrate called MacLennan's boss but received a cool response: as far as the district commander was concerned, the inspector should leave with as little fuss as possible.

The magistrate thought MacLennan deserved a sympathetic ear and he turned to Hong Kong's champion of the underdog, Elsie Elliot. (She later married and became known as Elsie Tu, as she will be referred to hereafter.) The urban councillor was distrustful of the police. She had come to Hong Kong in the 1960s, when the force was riddled with corruption, and despite pushing for an anti-corruption watchdog, she remained sceptical of the police. If anyone would see that justice was done, it was Elsie Tu. MacLennan hinted that the allegation might have been triad-instigated and told Tu about the files he had seen in Special Branch. Tu was in a unique position—not only did she have a big heart, she also had the contacts needed to make things happen. She wrote to the Governor, who in turn called the police and was told the matter was being looked into. The Governor forwarded Tu's letter to the police; it arrived the same day as a memo from the Civil Service ordering the cancellation of MacLennan's dismissal because the Governor deemed it unfair.

MacLennan got his job back, but he had done himself no favours. The police like to sort out their own problems. By dragging in lawyers, magistrates, the governor, and Elsie Tu, MacLennan was seen as both a troublemaker and a cry-baby. Given its distrust of MacLennan, the SIU was happy to hear a report from its new informant, Fulton, about MacLennan. With barely concealed indignation, Fulton complained that MacLennan had made a pass at his boyfriend, Raymond.

Elsie Tu

This was just the opportunity Brooks and Quinn had hoped for. The police had been embarrassed by the botched attempt to sack MacLennan, and now was their chance for revenge. Meetings with informants were always informal, and it was over a beer that Brooks and Quinn told Fulton that they wanted him to get evidence to convict MacLennan. They asked him to introduce MacLennan to one of his gay friends and see if the inspector tried to make a pass at him. If he did, they would have their proof. Quinn suggested Fulton use his boyfriend because MacLennan had already shown an interest in Raymond. Fulton was outraged. He had made his complaint out of anger that MacLennan had dared to make a pass at his lover, and he did not expect to be asked to use Raymond as bait. Fulton said as much, but Brooks just laughed. If he was not careful, Brooks warned, they might just charge him. Fulton backed down and agreed to help, simply to end the meeting.

Brooks and Quinn met Fulton a week later. They were angry Fulton had done nothing about setting MacLennan up. They wanted results and they were pinning their hopes on him. Fulton was in a precarious position. As a known homosexual he was vulnerable, but he had no intention of going ahead with the plan and he plucked up the courage to say so. Quinn was furious. He looked Fulton up and down with naked disgust and snarled: 'You better f***ing watch out. Don't get too big for your boots'.

The meeting really shook Fulton up. A friend suggested he speak to the Police Commissioner, Roy Henry, as he suspected the SIU's demands were illegal. As Henry was widely rumoured to be gay, Fulton hoped he might get a sympathetic hearing from him. But he never saw the commissioner; his District Commander handled the matter. One phone call was all it took to tell Brooks to pick on someone else. Fulton was never used as an informant again.

With Brooks and Quinn off his back, Fulton felt obliged to warn MacLennan that the SIU had it in for him. He did not know MacLennan personally, but he knew the inspector had a good rapport with Elsie Tu, so he told her about how Brooks and Quinn had tried to push him into setting up MacLennan. Tu was angry. It was the kind of behaviour she expected of the police and she called the Attorney-General straight away. 'Why don't they go after some of the other police?', she complained. He asked to whom she was referring and when she told him it was the Police Commissioner, he simply said: 'Well, we often hear stories of that, but we have no proof.' Tu explained that she had heard that MacLennan was being framed and she thought that, as head of the Legal Department, the Attorney-General ought to know.

Fulton was not the only one Brooks and Quinn had been squeezing for information; they had done the same thing to Lui Man, a married bisexual constable. He had been transferred from the Special Investigation Unit a year earlier amid rumours that he had been passing information about raids to the gay community. Lui Man was terrified his wife would find out about his past and Brooks used this to pressure him into coming up with names of homosexuals. He called his former lover, Peter, whom he had known for ten years, and begged him for help. When Lui Man married, Peter had become a gigolo, and the officer knew his friend would be able to come up with some names. Peter was reluctant, but after a couple of days of pleading phone calls, he came up with two; one of these was MacLennan, known as 'Inspector John' among Tsim Sha Tsui's male prostitutes.

Brooks could not believe his luck. After pursuing MacLennan for months, his name had now fallen into his lap. He dragged Peter in for questioning and kept him in a cell overnight, pushing him to come up with names of gigolos. Peter resisted saying anything, but Brooks broke him down with a combination of threats and violence, and Peter gave him the names of eight male prostitutes. Over the next couple of weeks the rent boys were tracked down and brought in for questioning. The rule book went out of the window and Brooks and Quinn took it in turns to get confessions out of the youths. Eventually they all admitted MacLennan had paid them for sex.

Brooks now had all the evidence he needed, and the Legal Department gave him the go-ahead to prosecute MacLennan. He called the inspector's boss, Trotman, on 14 January 1980 and it was with satisfaction that he told him MacLennan would be arrested the following morning. If Trotman had kept quiet, events might have turned out differently, but he felt it only right to warn the inspector and give him a chance to get a lawyer.

When MacLennan found out Brooks was coming to see him the next morning, he went straight to the police mess and ordered a double vodka. The news did not come as a total surprise; Peter and two other gigolos had warned him that they had given his name to the police. He returned to the office, but a couple of hours later he was back in the mess, looking pensively out of the window over another vodka, when a friend asked what was wrong. MacLennan told him about Brooks's expected visit, the files he had seen at Special Branch, and how the SIU had it in for him. His friend suggested he get a lawyer and recommended the same one he had used over his dismissal.

The lawyer arrived a couple of hours later. After MacLennan had explained the situation, the lawyer called Brooks and asked if the arrest could be delayed until the afternoon. Brooks was livid; he had spent months working towards this moment and he had wanted it to come as a surprise. He definitely didn't want a lawyer sitting in on it. MacLennan had caused a ruckus the last time he was in trouble and it appeared he was doing it again. Brooks made it clear he had no intention of changing the arrest time to suit the inspector. The lawyer arranged for a colleague to be with MacLennan in the morning and told the inspector to rest well. He would do his best to sort out the problem.

It would take a year and HK$16 million to determine what happened after MacLennan's lawyer left. In the morning, Quinn and Brooks waited for MacLennan in Trotman's office and when he failed to appear they went to his flat, a ten-minute walk away. The building's manageress gave Quinn a skeleton key, but the door had been locked from the inside, and he and Trotman had to smash a hole through it to get in. The curtains were drawn and the flat was in darkness. Quinn turned on the light. The furniture was standard government-issue fare, a free-standing fan towering over the bookshelf where a dozen wine bottles were displayed like trophies. On the edge of the desk lay a brief note in spidery handwriting. It read: 'Please, please tell my family this was an accident and that I was a good officer.' It was signed with MacLennan's initials and dated to the nearest minute: '0610 hours, 15.1.80'.

Quinn and Trotman tried the bedroom door, but that too had been locked from the inside. They prised it open with a crowbar. From the doorway they could see MacLennan sprawled on his back, a gun lying next to his foot. He was fully dressed and five dark stains had seeped through his shirt. There was no doubt in Quinn's mind that MacLennan had committed suicide. He was so sure that he did not even bother to call in a homicide team. Neither did he check MacLennan's hands for gunpowder. A simple test was all it would have taken to determine whether the inspector had shot himself.

Elsie Tu read the headlines with horror the next morning, then she read between the lines. She was convinced MacLennan had been killed. She had spoken to Fulton only days before about the SIU's plot to frame MacLennan and refused to believe he could have shot himself five times. Elsie Tu certainly was not the only one who was suspicious, but she was among the most vocal. MacLennan's body was cremated just a day after his death. Tu expressed disgust at what she saw as the police bullying of his parents into giving permission for a cremation and the 'unholy haste' of his funeral.

The coroner refused to consider charges of a government frame-up. He insisted such matters were out of his terms of reference and that an inquest was limited to evidence of how, where, and when a person died. But his dismissal of what many saw as the key issues fuelled public debate. *Open Line*, a radio talk show, became a hotline for speculation and dissent. The founder of the Samaritans was invited onto the show. He refused to accept that MacLennan had killed himself and insisted a person would be psychologically destroyed after shooting himself once in a dark room. He certainly would not have been able to do it five times. Gay police and gigolos called into the show to talk about how they had been hounded by the Special Investigation Unit. The anonymity of the programme made it an ideal forum for debate; it was the first time homosexuality had been so widely and openly discussed in Hong Kong.

After nine days in court, the inquest jury were not convinced that MacLennan had killed himself and produced an open verdict—they could not say with certainty that he had taken his own life. The verdict did nothing to allay suspicions and the talk of cover-ups and set-ups spread beyond Hong Kong's borders. The *New Statesman* heated up the debate: 'The dead inspector was probably not a homosexual at all. He had been the victim of a homosexual frame-up attempt two years before, which had failed...the most likely motive for the MacLennan murder would have been the knowledge he acquired of the whole conspiracy during his service with the local Special Branch.' The pathologist was quoted by the *Spectator* and his uncertainty did little to quell the speculation: 'I cannot say whether the wounds were self-inflicted or done by someone else. All I can say for certain is that it was not by accident.'

John MacLennan's death became an international issue. Labour Members of Parliament, Robin Cook and Robert Parry, spoke out, voicing Britain's concern, and the Scottish Homosexual Rights Group demanded an immediate public inquiry. Under pressure to re-open the inquiry, the Attorney-General called a press conference. He said he did not doubt that MacLennan had committed suicide and that the matter should be put to rest. He made no mention of the open verdict and was taken to task over his omission. The press demanded to know whether or not he was overriding the jury and Elsie Tu was incensed: 'How dare he say the jury is wrong—what is the purpose of having a jury if he doesn't want to hear the results?'. Public outrage and fierce press coverage forced the Attorney-General into a corner and six months after MacLennan's death a commission of inquiry was set up.

Pimps, prostitutes, and police were hauled onto the witness stand and Fulton, among others, was questioned in intimate detail about his private life. The trial was an ordeal for Fulton. His boyfriend was labelled a prostitute and lawyers enjoyed a number of jokes at his expense. 'Have you seen the scene in *Boys in the Band* where they say "show me a happy homosexual and I'll show you a corpse"?,' quipped one barrister. There were plans to highlight the hypocrisy surrounding the MacLennan case by exposing the Police Commissioner as a homosexual, but Justice Yang (who later became the Attorney General) put a stop to that. He refused to allow anyone to ask the commissioner personal questions.

After a year of investigations, interviews, and tests, the inquiry concluded that MacLennan had committed suicide. The 400-page report sold out within a few hours. Everyone was intrigued to hear the answer to the burning question: How could someone shoot himself five times in the chest?

It was thought that MacLennan had held the muzzle of the gun, a .38 Smith & Wesson, against his chest and pulled the trigger with his thumb. All five wounds were contact wounds and the last shots were grouped so closely together that it was more likely that MacLennan had held the gun close to his chest and fired repeatedly than that he had been shot from a distance. A firearms expert said that even if the first shot had been fatal, MacLennan could have remained conscious for twenty to thirty seconds, which would have been long enough to fire another four shots. But it appeared that the final shot was the fatal one; it had pierced his heart. The first four bullets had not hit a single major organ.

There was much debate about whether the force of firing the gun would have thrown MacLennan or whether the gun would have leapt from his hands. The expert said that the gun which MacLennan had used produced very little recoil, enough to cause a man to sway, but not enough to throw him. To prove his point, he suspended two 16-kg blocks of gelatine, simulating the texture of the body, from the ceiling and used MacLennan's gun to fire into the blocks. The gunshots caused the gelatine to sway a couple of inches and, considering that MacLennan was not freely suspended, it was thought that he would have moved even less.

There were other factors that pointed to suicide, the main one being that all the doors and windows had been locked from the inside. Elsie Tu had claimed that an assailant might have shot MacLennan, hidden in the wardrobe, and escaped during the chaos of the discovery of the body, but this theory was dismissed—surely a lone gunman would have been spotted fleeing the scene.

MacLennan's last hours were pieced together. After he had seen his lawyer in the mess, he had had a couple more drinks and then gone home. At 2am he had requested a wake-up call for 5.30am and the duty officer who made the call said MacLennan sounded tired and confused. Twenty minutes later, MacLennan rushed into the report room and said he was going on a raid and needed a gun. He barged into the armoury and was so impatient that he made a couple of mistakes as he filled out the register; he put his signature in the wrong place and recorded the wrong time. MacLennan was issued a

.38 Smith & Wesson and hurried back to his flat. Half an hour later, five shots rang out. The gunfire woke one of his neighbours, but she assumed the noise was firecrackers and went back to sleep.

Twenty years after MacLennan's death, Elsie Tu is still reluctant to accept that the inspector took his own life. The evidence points to suicide and, when pushed, she accepts this, but even so she insists it was a murder of sorts: 'He was potentially murdered in so far as he hadn't a way out, he was pushed into killing himself.'

Serial Killers

In 1978, the FBI coined the term 'serial killer'. The first Hong Kong man to fall into the category was Lam Kor-wan, a taxi driver better known as the Jars Killer, because he pickled the body parts of his victims in Tupperware containers. Lam went on a killing spree during 1982 and 1983. A decade later, Lam Kwok-wai's series of rapes and murders terrified women throughout the territory.

It is sheer coincidence that Hong Kong's only two known serial killers were both surnamed Lam (a common Chinese surname), but it is probably no coincidence that both were loners. It was not so much that they had rejected society—society had rejected them. They simply did not fit in. It is tough to be alone in Chinese society, especially in Hong Kong, where everything is based around group activities. Social occasions demand large gatherings of family and friends—the more the merrier, the noisier the better. If someone remarks that a restaurant is noisy, the comment is treated as a compliment because in Chinese culture the happier people are, the more noise they make.

Both murderers were loners. They were alienated from their peers and isolated from their families, even though they lived with them. The Jars Killer lived with his family in a tiny flat, sharing a room with his younger brother. Yet despite this enforced intimacy he managed to bring death, dismemberment, and necrophilia into the home without his family's knowledge. Hong Kong's other serial killer, the 'Tuen Mun Rapist', also lived at home. Divorce and alcoholism had broken up his family and days would pass without a word being exchanged. Unemployed and out of touch with his peers, he sought refuge in alcohol, as his father had done, until he began raping and murdering.

Both killers desperately needed friendship, but the intimacy they sought eluded them. It would be easy to dismiss their hunger as purely sexual, but the truth is far more complex. They were guilty of horrific acts of violence and yet in the end both revealed a shy vulnerability, a desperation that seemed at odds with their crimes.

3

Lam Kor-wan: The Jars Killer

The photo technician did a double take when he saw the pictures. They were nothing like the snapshots he usually processed. It was not the first time he had seen shots of a naked woman; some were of her whole body, others close-ups. Her poses were deliberately pornographic, as though staged to mimic a pornographic magazine. Normally he would have dismissed the pictures as another batch of snaps from a couple's naughty photo session, but there was one he could not ignore. It was of a severed breast.

Within a couple of hours the film was in the hands of the manager of the Kodak shop. He took one look at the breast and called the police. A pathologist confirmed their fears that the woman in the photo was probably dead. He pointed out an injury on the inside of her thigh where her creamy skin was marked by a dark red blotch. It looked as though she had been burnt.

Picking up the photographer would be easy because the film was due for collection the following day. On 17 August 1983, two plain clothes officers waited outside the shop in Tsim Sha Tsui. They sat there all morning and afternoon, warily eyeing everyone who went in. It was early evening when a taxi pulled up to the curb and the driver ran inside. As soon as he handed over his receipt the cashier signalled the police. This was the man they were looking for. He was in his early twenties and casually dressed in jeans and a T-shirt. They waited for him to pay for the film and arrested him as he walked out. He insisted that the pictures were not his; he was merely collecting them for a friend. The police did a rough search of the taxi and found a knife tucked under the sun visor. In some cases a knife might be a crucial piece of evidence, but in this case it was just the tip of the iceberg. They were about to uncover perhaps the most gruesome series of murders in Hong Kong's history. An officer thumbed through the man's wallet and dug out his ID card; his name was Lam Kor-wan.

Half an hour later, the two officers and Lam stood on a busy street corner in To Kwa Wan, just north of Tsim Sha Tsui. They suspected that Lam's talk of a friend was a lie, but gave him the benefit of the doubt. After an hour's wait, it was obvious there was no friend and they walked him to his home a few streets away. Lam's mother, father, and younger brother looked up from the dinner table in surprise when the officers came in. The flat was a typical Hong Kong home, about 800 square feet with a tiny kitchen and two bedrooms, one of which Lam shared with his brother. The entrance to their room was obscured by a black screen made up hundreds of black film canisters stuck onto strips of adhesive tape and hung from the door frame. The plastic containers clattered as the officers brushed them aside.

The bedroom was tiny and dominated by a bunk bed, leaving a narrow passage, just a yard wide, to stand in. Given the size of the room, there was an incredible amount of things packed into it; every available space had been used for storage. A large box under the bed caught the eye of one of the officers and he dragged it out. It was an old ammunition box, about 15 by 30 inches. He recognized it as the box in the photos; it had been used to support the woman's hips. While he checked the box against the photos, the other officer asked Lam to unlock a chest. Inside were two Tupperware boxes, each about the size of a large cake tin, one rectangular, the other square. They were heavy and the officer put them on the floor and carefully removed from one the band of masking tape around the rim. As he peeled back the plastic lid the smell of formaldehyde hit him. Suspended in the clear liquid was a flesh-coloured object. He looked closer and discovered it was the severed breast.

They were left in little doubt that they were standing in a slaughterhouse. It took half an hour for homicide detectives to arrive and they began removing the boxes and trunks from the bedroom. When the forensic chemist, Sheilah Hamilton, arrived soon afterwards, she was struck not by the number of people crammed into the room, nor by the boxes scattered on the floor, but by the silence. There was usually a lively banter between the detectives, but this time they were struck dumb. Everyone was astounded by the amount of camera equipment: stacks of tripods, dozens of lenses, cases of lighting equipment, high-tech gadgets, an infra-red camera, even a photo enlarger. In the eerie silence Sheilah Hamilton unsealed the second

Tupperware box. What she saw would stay with her forever—no one there that night would be able to forget the freakish image of the severed breast, and inside the other box was a vagina, it too pickled in formaldehyde. A cursory inspection of the trunks and boxes revealed a huge stash of pornography, stacks of magazines and hundreds of photos.

It would take weeks to analyse and catalogue the evidence. The flat was sealed off for three days while the police searched it methodically. Even the floor was vacuumed and the scraps and small particles analysed; the forensics team found shavings of pubic hair in the debris. There was nothing unusual about that, except that the hair was neither Lam's nor his brother's. It wasn't until a week later that the detectives discovered whose hair it was. The bedroom was scrutinized and small flecks of blood were found on the walls. The police eventually seized 696 colour negatives, 1,500 colour slides, and 1,900 photos, predominantly pornographic. But the videos were the most disturbing. The tapes showed savage butchery and necrophilia and were considered too horrific for female eyes. Sheilah Hamilton was taken off the case.

The detectives sized up Lam Kor-wan, his father, and brother. They appeared to be a family of sex killers. The haul of body parts and pornography was phenomenal and it was unlikely that one person could keep such a hoard secret in so small a flat. The three men were taken to the station for questioning. Interviewed individually and kept in separate cells, all three denied any knowledge of the photos or body parts. There was no call for rough treatment. The detectives were in no hurry and the women—it certainly looked as if they were dealing with more than one woman—were already dead. These men were going nowhere until they came up with some answers, so they left them in the cells overnight. The police can detain suspects for forty-eight hours before charging them, but they had no need to worry about running out of time; they got their answer the next day.

Lam Kor-wan asked to see his brother first thing in the morning. Handcuffed, with a guard at either side, his brother was led into the interview room. As soon as he saw Lam he began screaming at him. He lashed out at Lam, hitting and kicking him as much as his handcuffs would allow. Lam tried to fend off the blows but it took two officers to wrestle the brothers apart. When Lam had caught his breath, he shouted to be heard over his brother's rage: 'Don't worry, I'll tell the truth.'

The truth proved to be Hong Kong's most disturbing murder story to date. Lam showed no emotion as he recounted the killings. After a few days of answering questions matter-of-factly, he asked one of the detectives to bring him his electronic chess set. Playing calmed his nerves and he was good at it. Much of Lam's childhood had been spent glued to the black-and-white chequered board, his surrogate 'best friend'. School had been a lonely experience, he was shy, and he had never lost his nervous edge.

The police seized a phenomenal amount of pornography. The magazines had been sent from Britain by mail order, as Lam had been too embarrassed to buy them over the counter. His stash was kept locked up and even his brother had no idea about it. The magazines, like all of Lam's possessions, were filed away with obsessive neatness. All his LP records were diligently catalogued—there was no listening to an album and tossing it carelessly aside. One day he had caught his brother looking at one of his records, became furious, and hit him; Lam could not bear anyone trespassing on his privacy.

Although they shared a room, it was not as difficult as it might seem for Lam to keep such sordid secrets from his brother. He had always worked the night shift, which meant he saw almost nothing of his family. When he got up they had already left for work and when he returned home at about 5am, they were in bed. They knew about his fascination with photography, but they never suspected that when he locked himself in his room he was creating his own porn studio. Lam would re-photograph pictures from girlie magazines, strapping a camera onto his enlarger and making the pictures life-size. His hobby took up much of his free time and he invested thousands of dollars in equipment. But eventually he tired of the game. He wanted to get closer to the real thing.

After weeks of toying with the idea, he bought a Polaroid camera and began sneaking into women's toilets. It was the late 1970s and most public toilets in Hong Kong were little more than a hole in the floor. Holding his camera under the cubicle door, Lam would snap a shot and then run. He angered and humiliated dozens of women, but after a few months he gave up the practice because he was afraid of the irate women who chased him out of the toilets.

On 3 February 1982 Lam became more than just a voyeur. It was close to 4am and he was driving, as usual, around Tsim Sha Tsui looking for customers. He picked up a woman outside a restaurant and it was immediately obvious that she was drunk. Part way into the journey she told Lam to stop and when he pulled up at a petrol station, she threw open the door and vomited. Slamming the taxi door shut, the woman told him to go in the opposite direction. Lam did a U-turn, but a few minutes later she changed her mind again.

Something in Lam snapped; he had had enough. He pulled into a lay-by, still in Tsim Sha Tsui, went around to the passenger door, and, using a length of electrical wire, strangled the woman. He drove home and parked, as he usually did, outside his flat. It was 5am, about the time that he normally finished his shift. The street was deserted, so he took his chance and carried the woman across the street and into his block of flats. The night watchman was asleep on a camp bed in the lobby and did not stir as Lam hurried past. He let himself into the flat as quietly as he could and hid the body under the sofa. For several hours he lay in bed feigning sleep. As he listened to his brother and parents get up and have breakfast, he thought about his next move. When he was sure they had left, he got up and began his preparations. He covered the strip of floor in his room with plastic, making sure that even the skirting boards were protected. Then he laid the body on the plastic and locked the bedroom door.

Using an electric saw, he began to cut up the body. Although he tried to be careful, it was impossible to stop some blood splattering against the walls. It took several hours to carve up the body, and he took photographs as he worked. When he had finished he wrapped up the head, limbs, and torso in separate parcels. He cleaned up meticulously, rolling up the sheets of plastic and carefully sponging the walls and floor. Taking the body down to his taxi took several trips, but no one paid any attention to the small packages he loaded into the boot. Satisfied that he had left no hint of his butchery, he drove to the New Territories. He was desperate to find an isolated place to dump the body and stopped when he found a deserted spot on the edge of the Shing Mun River, near Sha Tin. Making sure that no one was watching, he took the parcels out of the boot one at a time and threw them in the river. The muddy brown waters carried the parcels out to sea.

Lam never explained why he took the films to Kodak to be developed. One detective suggested he got a kick out of the risk of being caught—and once he nearly was. When he went to collect the photos he was pulled to one side and questioned about the dismembered limbs and cross-sections of joints. Lam said he was a university lab technician and that the photos were part of his medical research. The excuse was good enough and nothing more was said.

A little more than a week after the murder, Lam heard a news report of an arm washing up on the bank of the Shing Mun River. The following day a pair of legs was discovered and before long the rest of the body was found. The police did calculations based on the tides to try to work out what day the body had been dumped in the river. They scanned the missing persons reports, but had insufficient evidence to make a match. Only seven months later, when Lam confessed, were the police able to identify the woman. Her name was Chan Fung-lan, she was only twenty-one, and had been the manageress of the Chinese Palace Nightclub in Tsim Sha Tsui. After work she had gone for a few drinks and a late-night snack with her sister and two other bar workers and then caught a taxi home—Lam's taxi.

Lam Kor-wan's first murder may have been an opportunistic killing, but his next was planned. He was a perfectionist and was determined to be better prepared. Rather than use the crude electric saw, he wanted professional equipment and went to a surgical supplies shop. He pored over the knives and studied the blades and scissors, eventually buying some specialist surgical instruments and several bottles of formaldehyde. Three days after he had bought his supplies, Lam killed again. His second victim was a bar worker as well, but this time he was not as panicky. He strangled the thirty-one-year-old , again with an electrical cord and then took her home. Again he lay in bed waiting for his family to go to work before he could begin carving up the body.

Lam had spent days thinking about what he would do and he carefully set up the room exactly as planned. Before he went to work, he placed a tray under the body to catch the blood and stop it spilling onto the floor. He secured his video camera to a high corner shelf and pressed 'record'. The video he made showed him having sex with the body of the dead woman. Lam was a virgin; necrophilia was his first sexual experience. Later, studying the video footage, detectives realized he had taken the tray from the bottom of the family's budgie cage. They returned to the flat and seized it as evidence.

Lam had cut up the body with meticulous care. When the body was found and taken for autopsy, the pathologist remarked on his surgical skill; his incisions were so precise it looked as though he been professionally trained. The dismemberment complete, Lam again photographed the body parts.

He had spent a long time thinking about where to dump the body and after a number of midnight excursions he found a good spot. This time wrapped the body up in sheets of plastic. He put it in the boot of his taxi and in the early hours of the morning took the cross-harbour tunnel to Hong Kong Island. The spot he had in mind was a twenty-minute drive east of the city centre, on Tai Hang Road. He parked in a dimly lit section of the road which could not be overlooked by the nearby flats. The body was cumbersome and he struggled to get it out of the boot and carry it the short distance to the low railing. He dumped it over the side and watched as it rolled down the slope and lodged in a deep rain gully.

Over the next few weeks Lam continually played over the night's events in his mind. He was not plagued by guilt, rather by a determination to perfect his crime. Two months later he struck again. This time his victim was a cashier, her name Leung Sau-wan. He strangled her and brought her to his room in much the same way as the others. Lam wrapped up the body as before and returned to Tai Hang Road to dump it. He did not have sex with her body and was embarrassed when the police questioned him about the necrophilia on the video. He said he had only done it once and that he had no interest in the women sexually. The detectives pushed him to explain himself and he said he had made the videos because he 'wanted the world to see them'. He even 'groomed' the women's pubic hair, which explained the clippings the police collected in his room.

With each murder Lam became more adventurous and he spent his time carefully plotting his next killing. He was very familiar with Tsim Sha Tsui's bar area and knew the places where women would often wait for a taxi alone. His first three victims had all been what he called 'bad girls', and he told the police he felt no remorse about killing them because they were 'useless to society'. But for his next victim he wanted a better class of woman and deliberately chose an innocent-looking girl. Her name was Leung Wai-sum, she was only seventeen, and a virgin. Lam picked her up from outside a hotel in Tsim Sha Tsui. She had been at a sixth-form party, but decided not to go on with her school friends after the meal. They put her into a taxi to make sure that she got home safely.

Lam drove her down a quiet side road and parked. The girl was terrified when he grabbed her and handcuffed her to the front seat. It was only 9.30pm and too early to return home, but that was not the only reason he kept her hostage in his taxi. He wanted to talk to her. Starved of friendship and desperate for company, he kept her handcuffed for hours, asking her about her family, religion, and life in general. Lam enjoyed her company, but it was not enough to hinder his macabre plan. At about 4am, she fell asleep and Lam slipped the electrical cord around her neck and strangled her. He took her home and cut up her body as he had the others. While he was setting up the lighting equipment to film his activities, a lamp fell on her thigh and burnt her leg. This was the mark that the pathologist had noticed in the photographs.

Lam agreed to show the detectives where he had hidden the bodies. The second and fourth victims were where he had dumped them on the hillside, but he could not find the third. Dozens of officers combed the hill for days but their search produced nothing. A few months later, in December, a cleaner discovered a skull in a nearby park. Clean aside from some hair and two teeth, the skull had been found by a dog and abandoned in the park, surmised the detectives. To determine whether it was Leung Sau-wan's, an X-ray of it was superimposed over a photograph of the woman. There was no doubting the match: it was Leung Sau-wan's skull.

Lam passed the time before his trial with his electronic chess set. Only when absorbed in the game did he feel at ease. He told the police he felt no guilt about what he had done, although he did feel sorry for his last victim, the teenager. He even cried a little over her, but if there was any sign of emotion as he sat in court, it was difficult to tell what he was really thinking. He had a slight cast to his face. His mother testified that her husband had beaten both her and Lam when they lived in Malaysia. When they moved to Hong Kong, the abuse stopped, but Lam was already in his late teens. His father's temper was so bad that one day he had hit Lam so hard that he had lost consciousness. Many serial killers have suffered a serious head injury and more than one officer was to wonder whether he had been hit so hard that his brain had been damaged.

The necrophilia, pornography, and murders were deemed too disturbing for women, and an all-male jury was elected. They were shown the hundreds of exhibits and had to watch hours and hours of Lam's videos. The evidence against Lam Kor-wan was overwhelming and on 8 April 1983, he was sentenced to death.

While Lam went to prison for the rest of his life, his family, too, was also sentenced to its own form of punishment, one that would haunt them every day. Anywhere in the world it would be difficult to sell a flat that had been used as a slaughterhouse, but in superstitious Hong Kong the chances of selling the apartment were nil. There was little they could do to escape the cruel legacy of Lam's crimes, which condemned them to live for many more years with the constant reminder of what their own son had done. All they could do was hang the image of Chung Kwei (Zhong Kui), the Chinese exorcist and protector god, above the front door of the flat in the hope of chasing away evil spirits.

Tuen Mun: Cemeteries with Lights

You are never alone in Hong Kong. Almost everywhere you go, there is bound to be someone watching. Thousands of people are tucked into the city's dank crevices; they live crammed into high-rise buildings, often three generations under one roof. But Lam Kwok-wai felt alone.

To him every day felt much the same, but 24 April 1992 would be different. Lam lolled in bed with nothing to do but stare at the ceiling. The room was damp and a fan beat the stagnant air, bittersweet with the smell of stale sweat. He peered over the side of the bunk. His brother's bed was empty. He left the flat and passed through the corridor, which was thick with the musty aftertaste of burning incense sticks. He punched the lift button and let out a long, weary sigh. It was not the sigh of the sleep deprived, but of boredom, the exhaustion of doing nothing. The lift lobby was much like a multi-storey car park, the floor number branded on the wall in bold, black letters.

Lam walked aimlessly, for the sake of walking, for the sake of doing something. The boredom was becoming intolerable; his days were a listless monotony. There was little point in getting up early when there was nothing to do, nowhere to go. Some days he walked through the cityscape for hours. Tuen Mun had little to offer by way of excitement, and even less for those without money.

Tuen Mun was a late-1970s dream town. In the far west corner of the New Territories, closer to the border with mainland China than Central, it was to be a new, self-sufficient satellite town. The lofty plans of distant architects envisaged a town in which 'its citizens will enjoy a life with some dignity and a little more spaciousness than is possible elsewhere in Hong Kong'. Sadly, the reality did not match the promise and Tuen Mun's people became labelled by critics as 'citizens of cemeteries with lights' for the bleakness of their cityscape.

The first residents moved into Tuen Mun's public housing estates in 1978, but two years later the Mainland's first Special Economic Zone stole the limelight. Shenzhen lured factories across the border with cheap labour, and with the factories went the jobs. Residents of Tuen Mun became commuters, and the dream of self-sufficiency was already flawed.

Many youths just milled around, sitting in clusters in the parks, their cigarettes glowing in the dark. Tuen Mun's angry young men were Lam's peers. When he was fifteen, he had sat with them, tried marijuana, and taken slugs of cough mixture. But he preferred alcohol because it took the edge off his boredom and it was easier to kill time in a stupor. He had indulged in the usual teenage maladies: shoplifting, gang fights, and the like. Once he had chased a dog, run it into a corner, and stoned the animal to death—anything to break the gnawing boredom.

That was all years ago. He was twenty-one now, but little had changed and he still lived at home. He had abandoned school when he began hanging around in the park. Work came sporadically. He was a decorator, and although he was thin, shifting heavy boxes and furniture had toned his muscles and he was surprisingly strong. Gambling helped stave off the boredom as well, and late-night card games had whet his appetite for the casinos of Macau, but those trips were rare; serious gambling was not a kick he could afford. Illegal road racing was easier to arrange. The risk and concentration broke the spell of boredom and was a welcome adrenaline hit. The races gave him a sense of power: he was in control and determined to win, to prove himself at something, and earn respect. He took risks and was good at racing. That counted for something and helped lift him above the restrained silence of home life.

Home was a 450-square-foot flat that he shared with his father, stepmother, and four brothers and sisters. It was not a comfortable intimacy. The family lived in a silence that was broken only by the monotonous drone of the television. His father sat in front of the box and drank himself into a stupor every night. Silence was a means of coping with the lack of space and days would go by with little more than a few words exchanged.

It is easy to forget Tuen Mun as it was before the bulldozers moved in. Swathes of concrete had smothered vast tracts of country land, as if denying the past. More than 100 years ago, Tuen Mun provided the perfect retreat for conspirators attempting to overthrow the Ch'ing (Qing) dynasty. The same remoteness that attracted conspirators drew the enthusiasm of 1970s town planners, eager to develop the area and exchange the frugal agricultural life for one more in line with a modern Hong Kong. It was an ancient port and fishing village and before the architects put pen to paper the area had embraced thirty villages. The new construction tried to work in harmony with the *feng shui* of the area, but sometimes produced paradoxes: the Tin Hau Temple, where local fishermen worshipped, was no longer on the coast but beached in a new urban area near the city centre.

On this April day, Lam's aimless walk took him towards the sea, over a bleak stretch of land reclaimed in the early 1970s and turned over for housing estates and industry. Among the estates on the stunted outcrop was Oi Ming Estate, another series of uninspired concrete structures. It was late and the streets were deserted, most people already tucked into the building's pockets. The hum of a taxi as it pulled up outside the estate caught Lam's attention. A door swung open and a young girl got out. She looked as though she was in her early twenties, but in fact she was nineteen and a virgin. Lam watched her walk quickly across the concourse. In a trance-like state, but with the conviction of someone who knew what he was doing, as though he had been waiting for her, he followed.

Her footsteps echoed in the cavernous foyer, an ugly grey chamber made worse by harsh fluorescent lighting. Given the thousands of people who traipsed through it each day, it was surprisingly soulless. There were no plants or decorations, the only flourish a notice board displaying a series of warnings. It could have been the entrance to a block in George Orwell's *1984*, the stench of boiled cabbage replaced with the lingering smell of sweat and stir-fry.

An anti-litter poster taped to the rough wall depicted a pair of eyes, brows drawn together in a knot of disapproval. The caption read: 'Hong Kong is watching'. But no one was watching, no one saw the girl press the button to summon one of the four lifts, no one except Lam. He waited for the doors to jerk open and for the girl to get in, and then, just as they were closing, he jumped in after her.

As soon as the doors had shut, he swung around and grabbed the girl's throat, his fingers clasped around her neck. She struggled and he squeezed tighter, tiny blood spots forming in the whites of her eyes. The attack was frenzied and within seconds she had slumped to the floor. When she regained consciousness, she was lying in a pool of blood on the tiled floor of a stairwell. She was still dressed, but her shirt had been pulled up over her breasts, her jeans caught around her ankles. She had been raped.

After the assault, Lam had gone home. Trying not to wake his family, he had crawled into his bunk and fallen into a deep sleep. The weeks that followed were much the same as the previous ones, filled with the aching monotony of boredom, which he tried to relieve with alcohol. He sometimes drank wine, but preferred beer and brandy.

Two months after the attack on the nineteen-year-old, in June 1992, Lam again found himself wandering aimlessly. He had not woken until the late afternoon and, with nothing better to do, he took to the streets, trying to walk himself out of his colourless existence.

Close to 4.30am, he was walking past Tai Hing Estate when he saw a woman walking towards him. She was in her early thirties, short and plump. It wasn't until she was a few feet away that he decided to rob her. He kept his eyes on the pavement and as she passed he tried to snatch her handbag. Startled, the woman clutched her bag and jerked away from him. Impulsively, Lam grabbed her neck and throttled her until she lost consciousness. He quickly scanned the street—it was deserted. Holding the woman roughly under her arms, he dragged her into the lobby of a nearby building. There could easily have been someone waiting for the lift, a night worker much like this woman, who was a waitress at a club in Wan Chai. But the lobby was empty, filled only with the same bleak anonymity that pervaded the entrance of every estate. He hauled her past the lifts, to an alcove under the stairwell. There he raped her.

Two months later, in August 1992, Lam attacked again. This time the victim was a thirty-nine-year-old woman. She regained consciousness less than an hour later to find herself naked. She, too, had been raped.

The rapes continued, as did their frequency. Lam was now striking once a month, but his method did not waiver: the women were followed into a lift, strangled, dragged to a stairwell, and raped. His next victims were a thirty-two-year-old woman in September and a twenty-eight-year-old woman in October.

Rapes were not uncommon in Tuen Mun—there were sixteen reported in the area that year—but police began to recognize the pattern of blitz-like attacks in lifts and they suspected a serial rapist. There were no reported rapes between October 1992 and February the following year, but that did not mean he did not strike again. Chinese women are traditionally reluctant to report such assaults.

Lam woke late on 24 February 1993 and lay in bed for as long as possible, trying to deny the reality of his day, his existence. In the late afternoon, unable to bear the oppressiveness of the tiny flat any more, he went for a walk. He broke for a few beers, which he drank in a park, and when he felt he could walk no further, he caught a taxi.

Before he reached home, he noticed a few late-night hawkers and told the driver to stop. A handful of people clustered around the makeshift barrows, which offered the usual winter snacks: sweet potatoes, corn on the cob, and a thick offal broth. The warmth from the barrows and lively banter looked inviting, so he bought a snack and a couple of beers and sat on a nearby park bench. He ate without appetite and drank with similar reluctance, supping the beers slowly but steadily. He was still sitting there hours later, in a dazed stupor, when he noticed a woman walking across the park. She was alone and her vulnerability excited him. He wanted to have her.

The woman had spent the evening playing *mah-jong* with friends and they had seen her safely off in a taxi just after 4am. Perhaps her mind was still on the game, for she did not notice Lam following her. Fuelled by alcohol and driven by desire, he got into the lift after her. It was only when he spun around and clasped his hands around her neck that he realized she was older than he had thought. She was fifty. The attack was much the same as before, only this time he sodomized the woman as well. He unclipped her earrings and took her necklace and handbag.

It was not until the following day, hearing the news on the radio, that Lam realized he had killed the woman. The police may have been able to ignore a rapist, but they could not dismiss a killer. Their first step was to set up decoys, and policewomen posed as residents returning home late at night. Given that the pathologist had estimated it took the rapist less than five seconds to knock out his victims, and that the lifts took ten seconds to reach the first floor, the job was for volunteers only. The policewomen would have back-up, but they would be on their own in the lifts.

The computer system devised to track down Britain's Yorkshire Ripper was adopted, and although it had come a long way since being introduced in 1985, it still had flaws. The names of all the men in the

Tuen Mun area with a record of sexual offences were logged in, but Lam's name never surfaced. He had a clean record and he did not fit the common profile of a rapist; he was only twenty-one and lived at home.

Lam may have gone largely unnoticed outside Tuen Mun, his frenzied attacks the anguish of an isolated community, but timing and politics made an example of him. Hong Kong's last governor, Chris Patten, had recently arrived and various pro-democracy forces were flexing their muscles. Politicians wanted to make an issue of crime, and what better way than to focus on the largely neglected new town? The media whipped the public into a frenzy with coverage of the lone stalker. Knowing there was a sex killer on the loose, and most likely living among them, they reacted out of fear. Their angst found form in anger and they took to the streets, calling for better police protection and demanding that the killer be brought to justice. The demonstrations were unprecedented, such public displays of anger usually being reserved for economic concerns, such as stock market crashes. Politicians took easy swipes at the police, accusing them of not doing enough to catch the killer. Desperate to prove themselves, police arrested and charged a twenty-six-year-old electrician with rape. Only two days later, they were forced to admit they were wrong and drop the charges.

Lam felt the pressure, too. Watching the news at home early one evening, he saw a report of the murder, panicked, picked up the phone, and called his only friend. Wong Kwong-ching had been a school friend, but they had lost touch and he was surprised to hear Lam's voice.

'I've killed someone, it's on the news now,' Lam said. He could hear Wong's television in the background as a photo of the fifty-year-old victim flashed up on the screen. She may have been attractive in her youth, but now she looked dowdy.

'Do you like fifty-year-old women?' Wong asked. Lam snapped back, asking him what he should do, whether he thought he was mad. The conversation was surreal. Wong said he didn't know what to say, what to think, and hung up. But it wasn't easy to ignore the call, if Lam were telling the truth, and Wong knew he had a responsibility to do something. He fretted over the conversation. He didn't want to finger a friend and neither did he want to be involved. Police estimated that forty-odd neighbours had walked over the victim's bruised and battered body as it lay in the stairwell, but none had reported it because they didn't want to get involved. Wong felt the same; it was none of his business and he was angry with Lam for dragging him in. After hours of agonizing, he called the police hotline and made an anonymous suggestion. 'You should make the "photofit" thinner in the face,' he said, and rung off.

Less than a fortnight after the call, on 14 April, Lam struck again. This time he raped and killed a twenty-two-year-old disc jockey only a minute's walk from his home. He had gone drinking in Tsim Sha Tsui and was on his way home when he noticed her walking down the street alone. He had seen her before; she lived in the block next to his. This time the assault was more violent than before and he knew he had killed her.

The police were becoming a laughing stock. The killer was under their noses, yet they were no closer to catching him. Patrols were stepped up and the policewomen decoys continued, but without success. Police suspected the killer was a taxi driver, perhaps a Lam Kor-wan of the 1990s, and cabbies were called in for questioning, but the enquiries led nowhere. Even the taxi driver who had driven the disc jockey home agreed to be hypnotized. His recovered memories helped narrow the time of the attack, but provided little else. Background checks of the victims came up with nothing either. It appeared the killer was striking at random, making every woman in Tuen Mun a potential victim. Despite a special service to escort women home late at night, the climate of fear remained.

Press coverage and public demands made Lam nervous, and he decided to stay with his elder sister in Hung Hom for a while. On Kowloon side, halfway between Tsim Sha Tsui and the former Kai Tak Airport, Hung Hom is much closer to the buzz of the city. The district's northern part is dominated by industry and the south is largely residential. The move did nothing to alter Lam's lifestyle. He still got up late, drank to stave off the boredom, and walked the streets. Although living with his sister, he rarely saw her. She left early for work and would often be asleep when he returned from his wanderings. Days would pass without a word exchanged and he became increasingly lonely, an intolerable alienation. Drink could no longer fill the void and he craved company, the comfort of a friend.

After less than a month in Hung Hom, he found himself drunk and following a woman home. Again, he got into the lift with her and when the doors closed he put his hands around her neck, but instead of squeezing until she fainted, he spoke to her. He warned her to be quiet—if she said nothing, he would not hurt her. Only when she nodded did he release her, stop the lift, and usher her onto the stairwell.

He ordered her to strip and she cried as she undressed. Her boyfriend, whom she lived with, was only a minute away, but he had no idea of the danger she was in. Lam raped and sodomized her, then told her to get dressed. She fumbled into her clothes and made to run away, but he grabbed her arm and asked her to just stay and chat with him. She struggled free and then turned on him, slapping him repeatedly across the face. Lam flew into a rage, grabbed her around the neck, and smashed her head against the wall. She slumped to the floor, dead.

Two months later, Lam struck again, but this time the woman escaped with her life and struggled home. After less than a month, he was wandering the streets just north of his sister's flat when he spotted a young woman. It was 1.30am and the street was deserted. He quickened his pace and caught up with her, knocked her to the ground, and kicked her in the stomach. When he had beaten her into submission, he raped her on a wooden cart. As suddenly as the attack itself, his violence subsided and he said he wanted to chat. Terrified, the twenty-one-year-old nodded. 'Will you be my girlfriend?' he asked shyly. Again she nodded. Lam was elated, took out a packet of cigarettes, and offered her one. He suggested a date to the cinema and when she agreed he couldn't suppress his happiness. They arranged a time and a place for the following day.

'Please be there. I'm a mess in this old T-shirt and jeans but tomorrow you'll be proud of me,' he gushed. As soon as the woman returned home, she broke down in tears and told her mother-in-law what had happened. She was told to forget what had happened, pretend that it was just a bad dream, and not mention it to anyone. In Chinese culture, rape brings extreme shame; it is a humiliation to be kept hidden. Her mother-in-law did not want anyone in her family tainted by such violence.

But the woman did not want to forget. Rape is among the worst things that can happen to any woman, the brutal assault and memories of violence often take years, if not a lifetime, to heal. She wanted her attacker caught and brought to justice. If it had not been for her brother, a Correctional Services officer, she might never have reported the rape. She told him the following afternoon and he encouraged her to go to the police. With her brother standing by her side for support, she explained what had happened and told them about the bizarre request for a date. A plan was devised to catch the rapist. She would wait for him outside the cinema and when she saw him she would signal by scratching her head and he would be arrested.

A couple of hours later she was standing outside the cinema. Two policemen and her brother were watching a short distance away. As promised, Lam made his appearance. He was wearing a white shirt, albeit creased, black dress trousers, and leather shoes. As he approached, she tried to smile and scratched her head. Lam returned her smile and greeted her nervously. She scratched her head again, but still there was no response. Terrified, she screamed and Lam bolted. The officers gave chase, but it was her brother who caught up with Lam and wrestled him to the ground.

Later that day, in the interrogation room, he complained he would not have been caught if he had been wearing his trainers, rather than the leather shoes he had worn to impress the woman. Lam was the prime suspect in the spate of rapes and murders, and there were many on the force who wanted to beat a confession out of him. But the detectives handling the case were adamant he should be treated as a friend until he broke down and told all.

Lam cut a pathetic figure, slumped forward as though he could not tolerate the weight of his being, and his shoulders shook with the force of his crying. The officers spoke to him with an unfamiliar kindness; it seemed as though they genuinely cared, that they were his friends. For hours he stared at the wall, his eyes rimmed red from crying. Interrogation cells have few creature comforts, but Lam noticed nothing of the bleakness of the room; the attention of the officers was more warmth than he had experienced in a long time.

Lam took a deep breath, trying to control his sobs, and then he cried out: 'I did it—I raped those women, I killed three of them.' The confession over, he let out a gut-wrenching howl and fell to the floor, writhing about like a madman. His face was flushed and his eyeballs bulged in their sockets. He tried to speak through the agony of his contortions, his words a thick foam about his lips: 'I can see them. They are watching me. I can see their ghosts going around the table.' Lam hauled himself back into his chair, but a detailed confession would have to wait, for his eyes darted about the room, as though mesmerized by the spirits, and then he collapsed.

Lam eventually awoke to give a full confession and later to sit numbly through his trial. He neither forgot nor regretted the attentions of the officers who had nursed the confession out of him, and he begged them, his only friends, to visit him in prison.

The jury found him guilty of the murders and he was given three terms of life imprisonment. As his sentence was read out, Lam sat stroking the contours of his right thumb and forefinger, transfixed by his murder weapon. As though it were not part of himself, he had given it a name; it was his 'fork'.

Tuen Mun's tower blocks remain grimy chimneys wallowing in a stagnant backwater. Those who can have flown the concrete nest and couples are reluctant to settle in the isolated spot. Yet far from being a ghost town, the estates remain crammed with people eking out a living. Rapes still occur, but at least these days the lifts are fitted with security cameras.

Money Matters

Money is everything in Hong Kong. The city's entrepreneurial spirit has lined countless pockets and fed myriad dreams. While little time is spared for martyrs, tycoons are revered almost as gods. They represent the collective dreams of a city devoted to Mammon.

In the early 1980s, Hong Kong's leading businessman was George Tan. He was so successful that he was said to have the Midas touch. It was George Tan who fuelled Hong Kong's property market in the early 1980s. In 1979 he bought the property development company Mai Hon Enterprises for HK$700 million. He renamed it Carrian Investments and used it to buy Gammon House for HK$998 million. (The prestigious building in Central was later renamed Bank of America Tower.) Seven months later he resold Gammon House for a mind-boggling HK$1.68 billion.

His timing could not have been better. When he entered the property market in 1979, many foreign banks were eager to do business in Hong Kong. One of these was the Hong Kong branch of Malaysia's Bank Bumiputra; George Tan built his empire on the strength of loans from this bank. But that knowledge only surfaced much later. It took a murder to open up the Carrian can of worms and expose the illegal practices that built Carrian's wealth.

There is very little old money in Hong Kong—most success stories are just one generation from the rice paddies. With poverty as a potent driving force, thousands of people have elevated themselves beyond their wildest dreams. But the lust for money can create dark characters, like Wong Kwai-fun, who was arguably one of the city's most treacherous business people. He presided over a loan shark empire and gave his siblings key roles to ensure that he was not cheated. His heavy-handed tactics crippled families and drove others to suicide. This manipulative thug seemed capable of anything in his quest to make money.

Carrian: The Honest Banker

The rainy season in 1983 seemed endless. Vast swathes of the New Territories were submerged by torrential rains and in the north a banana grove was swamped. A path wove through the overgrown plantation, but it was flooded and the villagers who used the trail were forced to take another route. So it was on Monday 19 July that an elderly woman carefully negotiated her way around the back of the grove, through the tangle of trees. Her cautious passage blinkered her view and she did not notice the dead man until she was almost upon him. The body lay at the bottom of a slope, covered in leaves and twigs, the clothing snagged and torn. She stared at the man as she shuffled past; he had a babyish face, but must have been in his mid-thirties. There was no blood, aside from a few small scratches on his face and hands. His had not been a gory death. A white towelling cord was tied tightly around his neck.

It was dark by the time the police reached the body. There was no wallet that might help identify the man. The only clue was a Malaysian coin caught in the lining of his pocket. The investigation began the next morning. Chief Inspector Norrie MacKillop, a conscientious detective known for his no-nonsense approach, was put in charge. It soon became clear that identifying the body would not be the problem.

MacKillop was still scouting around the plantation when he heard that someone from Malaysia's Bank Bumiputra had been reported missing. He met the bank's assistant manager, Henry Chin, at the morgue. It may have been nervousness that made Chin sweat, but more likely it was the thick summer heat, so humid it was hard to breathe. He recognized the body as that of his colleague, Jalil Bin Hj Ibrahim, an assistant manager based in Kuala Lumpur. MacKillop phoned his office and requested a warrant to search the bank. The red

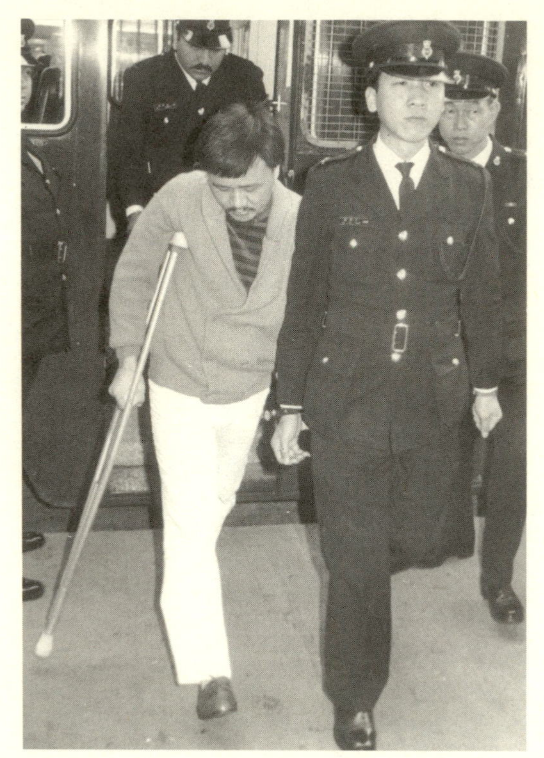

Mak Foon Than, injured after his failed attempt to escape

tape for warrants is laborious and he wanted to get the investigation under way as quickly as possible. He also requested that two Commercial Crime officers meet him at the bank; he wanted to make sure he had all the backing he might need.

MacKillop picked up the search warrant in the late afternoon of that day and headed straight for Bumiputra; it had already closed for the day and he was shown to Jalil's desk. The banker's diary was in the top drawer, and MacKillop flicked through the pages of meticulous notes. Each entry had been made with a steady hand, the letters formed with measured care. The journal reflected an ordered mind, the numerous notations suggesting a man who took his work seriously. The detective skimmed through the month of July. An entry from the previous Monday was a reminder to meet Tan Sri Ibrahim, a well-known Malaysian businessman, at the Regent Hotel to exchange US$4,000. There was nothing unusual about that. When important customers are in town, it is quite common for banks to send representatives to change their money personally. It was close to midnight when MacKillop decided to call it a day. He gave the diary to a Commercial Crime officer, Mike Rawlinson, to look over. Rawlinson was a quiet, well-informed man; his experience of crime was limited to the white-collar variety. Used to trawling through bank statements and accounts, he found the diary intriguing. In the early hours of the morning he called MacKillop, his voice thick with excitement. There were many dubious deals involving cheques, Rawlinson said, but Jalil's notes hinted at far worse.

MacKillop knew a little about Bank Bumiputra; it had been set up in the 1970s to help poor Malaysians gain ground against the country's wealthy Chinese and Indian communities—a bank designed to give Malaysia's needy a chance. Rawlinson filled him in on details he had gleaned from the diary and a couple of late-night telephone calls.

Jalil had been working for the bank in Kuala Lumpur for six years and had been to Hong Kong a number of times as part of an auditing team. He had been promoted recently and his new position, as assistant manager, made him responsible for loans involving a Hong Kong real estate company, Carrian. The property group was already under scrutiny by Hong Kong's anti-corruption watchdog, the Independent Commission Against Corruption (ICAC). The bank had given huge loans to Carrian, which was on the verge of collapse despite a number of attempts to save it. No more drawdowns were allowed on the group's loan facility without the permission of a special committee set up to deal with Carrian. The Supervisory Committee was headed by the bank's chairman, Lorrain Osmond, and included a number of other senior bank executives.

MacKillop was pleased to have someone else handle the commercial side, since finance was not his field and Rawlinson's unassuming manner and the ease with which he explained complex banking practices made him a good person to have around. Over the next few days, Rawlinson carefully examined Jalil's diary and personal letters. It soon became clear the banker had been in deep trouble. Jalil appeared to be scrupulously honest, a trustworthy employee and loyal citizen, and it seemed he had been worried about the huge exposures to Carrian. In a letter to his wife, he had hinted at his concern: 'I really don't know what to do. It will cause great embarrassment to the bank, but I also have a duty to King and country.' It looked as though Jalil had been sent to Hong Kong to stop any more money going out to Carrian.

Later the police found a personal file in which Jalil had written: 'The bank has been used and commissioned to make money for political ends...why should the country suffer because of their greed? I am just a small part of the deception. I want no more to lie and betray the bank and my family.'

Rawlinson suspected Jalil had known he was in a dangerous situation, but that there was little the banker could do. Jalil's brother-in-law in Malaysia echoed those fears. After dinner, on the eve of his departure, Jalil had told him he was in a difficult position at work and did not know what to do. His visit to Hong Kong must have been important because he had cut short a holiday with his wife and two young children to make the trip.

Rawlinson and the Commercial Crime team ploughed through documents at the bank, while MacKillop focused on the Regent Hotel, where Jalil had supposedly gone to meet the Malaysian businessman. The towelling cord used to strangle Jalil looked much like a bathrobe belt and MacKillop asked to see one of the hotel dressing gowns. It was a perfect match. This was a start, but even if the killer had stayed at the hotel, narrowing down the suspects from the hundreds of guests would not be easy. Three days had passed since the murder, and many would have left Hong Kong. The victim had been a foreigner, so it was quite possible the killer was a non-Hong Kong resident as well. MacKillop's team scrutinized airline passenger lists and hotel guest lists, unsure of exactly what they should be looking for, but searching for anything suspicious or names that might stand out.

Cross-checking hotel guest lists led to the first breakthrough. A Malaysian man named Mak Foon Than had booked into both the Regent Hotel and the Regal Meridian Hotel on 18 July. Double-booking is not unheard of, but this man had actually paid for both rooms. The Regent was among the first of Hong Kong's top hotels to install a sophisticated computer system. All bills were computerized, which meant credit card numbers were recorded and regular guests' spending history noted. Even such items as soap preference, room service, and room temperature could be traced. MacKillop introduced himself to the Regent's manager and explained the situation.

The manager dug out the hotel's record of Mak, who had taken room 609. MacKillop flicked through the file and broke into a broad grin when he spotted a brief notation: Mak had reported his bathrobe belt missing. It looked as though MacKillop was on the right trail, but he was still a long way from anything that would stand up in court. If it had been a stabbing, he might have found flecks of blood on the wall, but with a strangulation there was little chance of forensic evidence. Instead MacKillop pinned his hopes on the hotel staff and showed them photos of the two Malaysians to jog their memories. The manager remembered seeing them at about lunchtime on 18 July, when they had met in the lobby and walked through to the guest lifts.

Presumably, Jalil and Mak had gone to room 609, but it seemed they were not alone. The hotel's room service records that afternoon showed that refreshments were delivered for three people, not two. MacKillop interviewed the room boy who had delivered the teas and coffees. The boy said he had not gone into the room, but that the door was left ajar and from where he stood he had seen a briefcase lying open on the table, with a number of documents scattered around. The boy described the briefcase, stating that it was unlike either the one that the manager had seen Mak with in the lobby or the one Jalil used.

The bell boy also remembered Mak, because the Malaysian had asked him to carry a very heavy suitcase. It was too heavy for the bell boy alone and Mak had helped him carry it from room 609 to the taxi rank. With typical Regent efficiency, the cab's registration number was noted and MacKillop tracked down the driver, who also remembered Mak and his heavy suitcase—he had driven him to a few car hire firms. Mak rented a car, a Nissan, at the third company, and signed for it in his own name. MacKillop was in luck. The car hire firm not only had a copy of the agreement, but also a photocopy of Mak's passport.

While the detective was interviewing hotel staff, he ran a background check on Mak. The results came through over the next few weeks. Mak, it seemed, was a businessman who travelled frequently between Hong Kong and Kuala Lumpur. He had a wife in each city—a Malay woman in Kuala Lumpur and a Chinese one in Hong Kong—and had connections with the Malaysian Chamber of Commerce. He was also wanted in Malaysia for a minor assault a few weeks earlier.

As the information arrived, so did the evidence against Mak. The investigation was almost textbook perfect, but one thing failed to fit. On 18 July, the day Jalil went to the Regent, there was an important meeting at the Hilton Hotel. Carrian was on the brink of collapse and both angry creditors and Commercial Crime inspectors were closing in. Some of the main players in Carrian, including George Tan, Bentley Ho, the firm's executive director, and the bank's chairman, Osman, were at the Hilton for the make-or-break conference. The meeting was to obtain another US$1.4 million of their loan. It was a relatively small amount, but in the scheme of things it was crucial. The US$1.4 million had to be transferred to a holding account by the end of play that day or the rescue attempt would fail. Jalil had to authorize the loan but he had not been seen since the morning, when he went to exchange US$4,000 for a Malaysian businessman.

Jalil had called Henry Chin from the Regent in the early afternoon. He sounded much himself and said he would return to the bank within an hour. He told Chin that in the meantime he should not, under any circumstances, authorize a further withdrawal from the Carrian loan. But Jalil did not return to the bank, and he never made it to the meeting at the Hilton. Impatient to secure the loan, the Hilton group grew restless. George Tan called Chin every ten minutes to find out what was keeping Jalil. Chin had no idea; all he could do was try to pacify the men until Jalil turned up.

After a couple of hours of restless pacing, Tan and his Carrian partner, Bentley Ho, went to the bank themselves. They barged into Chin's office and handed him a note from Osman. Chin read the note aloud: 'Implement immediately'. Osman was not only the bank's chairman, but also a member of the Supervisory Committee for Carrian, which made him the only person besides Jalil who could authorize the loan. Chin played for time, hoping Jalil would come back to the office, or at least telephone. Jalil did call again, just before 4pm. Chin explained the pressure from Carrian to grant the loan, but Jalil was adamant that he should not give in: 'Whatever you do, don't authorize the drawdown. I'll be back soon.' Those were probably Jalil's last words, for as soon as he had spoken them, the line went dead. Chin was left clutching the receiver, wondering what had happened. When Jalil failed to call back, he crumbled under the pressure from Carrian and the chairman and granted the loan. The next time Chin saw Jalil was in the morgue.

MacKillop saw two possible motives for the murder. Jalil might have been lured to the Regent Hotel to be robbed of the US$4,000. The detective knew the currency exchange request was a hoax; he had spoken to Tan Sri Ibrahim, who told him he was not even in Hong Kong on 18 July. But if Jalil had been conned into going to the Regent merely to rob him, why had he been kept there all day? Jalil knew there was a crucial Carrian meeting at the Hilton, but even though it seemed from his first telephone call to Chin that he was free to leave the Regent, he did not. The more likely motive was that he had been killed to prevent him from blocking the drawdown, which would have ruined the last-ditch attempt to save Carrian.

As MacKillop closed in on Mak, the search warrant was kept open. The police seized the bank, and a uniformed officer stood guard outside as Commercial Crime inspectors sifted through confidential files, uncovering loans to Carrian worth billions of US dollars, enough to justify a raid on Carrian's offices. Relations between Britain and Malaysia had long been strained and the investigation did nothing to ease them. Malaysia complained that the officers were being overzealous, seizing bank documents for political reasons.

Jalil's murder made front-page news and the press eagerly followed the story. One Chinese newspaper not only caught onto Mak as a prime suspect, but also traced his wife to a flat on Tsing Yi Island, off the Kowloon Peninsula. MacKillop had intended to wait for more information before raiding the flat, but, fearing that Mak might run when he saw the newspaper coverage, he organized a raid for the next morning, 3 August. Mak's wife lived in a third-floor flat and police hammered on the front door just before 7am. When there was no answer, they tried to break it down. They were unable to budge the metal grille and it took them nearly an hour to saw through it. When it finally gave way, they barged into the flat in time to see Mak climbing out of a window. He shinned down a drainpipe, but in his haste to escape he slipped and fell. Mak was on his feet by the time police reached him, but he was doubled over in pain and was taken away in an ambulance instead of a police van.

Mak had broken a small bone at the base of his spine and another in his pelvis and was rushed into surgery. When he came to he was in the custodial ward, but doctors would not let MacKillop see him until the following afternoon, by which time Mak, with the benefit of painkillers, was in much better shape. Interviews were MacKillop's forte; he had mastered the knack of putting suspects at their ease and encouraging them to open up. This was a potentially complicated case, so he made sure everything was played by the book. He brought a Malaysian interpreter with him to translate, but he soon discovered Mak spoke fluent English, so the questioning was left to MacKillop.

There was no respite from the summer heat. Although the doors and windows were thrown open, the hospital ward was stifling.

MacKillop told Mak he was under arrest for Jalil's murder, but MacKillop wasn't worried about rushing into accusations or direct questions—he just wanted to get Mak talking. As Mak began to open up MacKillop let him talk freely, but he did throw in some questions, and the denials Mak gave reinforced his suspicion that Mak was guilty. He asked him, for example, whether he had ever driven in Hong Kong or if he had ever lent his driving licence or passport to anyone. Mak said no. Slowly the detective was closing off the bolt holes in preparation for some tougher questions the next day. The thirty-two-year-old Mak had a good sense of humour and proved a smart interviewee, charismatic and clever. While the detective was leisurely introducing key questions, Mak was working on his own agenda. As he talked about his business, he dropped hints about an argument with his wife, thus laying the foundation for an explanation as to why he was booked into two hotels.

MacKillop began the interview earlier the next day. The two had already developed a good rapport and Mak rambled on good-humouredly about his life and connections in Malaysia. After an hour, the detective threw in his first big question. 'Is this your signature?' he asked, showing Mak the car hire agreement. Mak stumbled over his words, admitted it was his signature, and offered a lame excuse. MacKillop refrained from a direct accusation, which Mak would simply have denied. Instead he wanted to build up a case through Mak's lies.

Mak was sitting up in bed when MacKillop arrived the following morning. He said he had done some serious thinking and wanted to level with MacKillop and tell him the whole story. The detective set up a tape recorder and sat on the edge of Mak's bed. It was not yet 11am but the heat was insufferable. The detective rolled up his shirtsleeves, uncovering a deep scar on his forearm.

Mak's tale began the night before he left Kuala Lumpur. He said he had had dinner with Malaysia's Finance Minister, Razaleigh, who had given him US$6 million in cash to pass on to some people at the Shangri-La Hotel in Hong Kong. Hinting that the money was a pay-off, Mak said he made the delivery and then moved on to the second part of his instructions, to meet a Korean man named Shin at the Regent Hotel. Shin told him to go to the lobby, meet Jalil, and bring him up to the room. Mak was vague about what happened in the room. The two men talked business for a while, he said, and then Shin told him to buy a suitcase from the shopping arcade downstairs.

MacKillop knew this was probably true. He had spoken to a cashier in the arcade who remembered a Malaysian man buying a suitcase in the late afternoon. The man had looked like Mak. There is nothing criminal about buying a bag, but it is a different story if you know it is to be used to transport a corpse. Mak's answer to the detective's next question was crucial. MacKillop asked him at what point he knew that Jalil would be killed. 'When the Korean told me to buy a suitcase,' Mak said. Knowing that Jalil would be killed and his body put in the suitcase made him an accomplice. Afraid that later, in court, Mak might argue that he had not understood the question, the detective put it to him another way. He asked what the bag was for. Without hesitation, Mak replied: 'To put the body in'.

As far as the detective was concerned, Mak had just sealed his fate. MacKillop knew he had Mak as an accomplice to murder, but he did not stop there. He asked Mak to describe the alleged Korean hit man. The Malaysian gave him a strange look, as if trying to recall an image, or perhaps to create one. Mak's gaze dropped to the detective's arm, and then he began a detailed description. 'He had a big scar on his arm,' Mak began. Immediately MacKillop sensed he was lying—he had caught him looking, fleetingly, at the scar on his arm and felt this was the springboard for a fictional hit man. But MacKillop let Mak continue. The Korean was a karate expert whom he had met in Libya, Mak said. MacKillop pressed him for more details and Mak obliged because it was in his interest to help if the Korean was the killer. Mak said he had been involved in a military deal with Shin and two brothers, surnamed Lo, who owned a textiles company. The detective pushed him to be more specific. Mak said they had met in the Shangri-La Hotel, and gave him a rough time frame.

The information was scant, but it was enough for MacKillop to try to track down the Korean. The Shangri-La records are kept in the hotel for a year and then stored in a warehouse. The detective sent a few of his men down to the warehouse, which was stifling, thick with dust, and without even a fan, let alone an air conditioner. While they trawled through thousands of reservations, bills, and receipts, MacKillop organized an identification parade at the hospital. The cashier at the luggage shop picked Mak out of the line-up as the man who had bought the suitcase, and the Regent's manager had no difficulty pointing him out as the Malaysian he had seen with Jalil in the lobby. The forensics team also had incriminating evidence. Fibres found on Jalil's suit corresponded with those taken from a suitcase of the same brand that Mak had bought. Mak was charged in hospital with aiding and abetting in Jalil's murder.

After days in the oppressive warehouse, MacKillop's men finally came across a record of Shin, the Lo brothers, and another Korean staying at the Shangri-La. MacKillop traced the Lo brothers to Los Angeles and flew there to interview them. There was no question of arresting the brothers—he merely wanted to substantiate Mak's story. The next stop was South Korea, to speak to Shin. The country was technically still at war with North Korea and getting permission for an interview was not easy. It was made even tougher by MacKillop's questions about military deals. After weeks of negotiations, the detective eventually found himself in a hotel room in Seoul waiting for Shin. The months of searching were close to an end and the few hours' wait to meet the Korean seemed an eternity.

As soon as MacKillop saw Shin, he had a gut feeling that the Korean was innocent. The introductions, under the unflinching gaze of the Korean police, were tense, but the atmosphere relaxed as Shin realized he was in no danger of being arrested; he was simply helping with an investigation. The outline of Mak's story fitted, but the essence of his version could not have been further from the truth. Shin was, as Mak had said, a karate expert, but so were thousands of Koreans. Far from being a professional hit man, he had a wife and children and worked as a toy salesman. He had met Mak a few years earlier and although they had discussed a deal with military implications, it had been for nothing more menacing than military surplus, haversacks, and the like. The deal came to nothing because Shin, deciding that Mak was a con artist, opted out at the last minute. As MacKillop suspected, Mak had transferred the blame onto a bogus Korean whom he had based on his knowledge of Shin.

Mak's trial dragged on for forty days, a long time, but nowhere near as long as the Carrian trial, whose repercussions were still being felt in Hong Kong's courts at the dawn of the new millennium. Most of the evidence against Mak was based on MacKillop's interviews with him in hospital. His defence fought to have the statements excluded and MacKillop was grilled on the witness stand for days. There were complaints that the interviews, which had averaged four hours, had been too long. And there were allegations that the detective had fabricated the links to Malaysia's Finance Minister—MacKillop would later laugh off those accusations, joking that he couldn't even spell Razaleigh's name at the time.

Mak gave his own evidence. He told the jury his wife had found out about his infidelities and he was certain she was taking her revenge. Fearing that the men pounding at the door had been sent by his wife to beat him up, he tried to escape by climbing out of the window. Mak insisted he had not killed Jalil; Shin was the killer. The case rested on the Korean, but MacKillop was having a hard time getting him onto the witness stand. Shin was happy to testify, but the Korean authorities were less keen. The mention of anything remotely connected with military deals was enough to set off alarm bells. The jury appeared undecided and it seemed Shin could swing the case. In the closing days of the trial, MacKillop's boss, Douglas Lau, was given permission to go to Seoul to try to persuade the authorities to let Shin give evidence. On the last day of the trial, Lau was given the green light and the witness was on the next flight to Hong Kong. As soon as his plane touched down at Kai Tak Airport, Lau took his statement and rushed it to court.

Shin's appearance in the witness box turned the trial around. He explained that he had been in Libya, was a karate expert, and had been involved with Mak, but that he regarded him to be a con artist. Mak's defence was already flagging and with Shin's evidence his case collapsed. Mak was sentenced to death for Jalil's murder.

If Mak was not the killer, but merely an accomplice, or even a pawn in a bigger plan, he could have struck a deal with the police. By telling them what he knew, he could have been granted a lighter sentence. But he did not. Off the record, insiders have said he may well have been told that if he said nothing his family would live. Mak received regular reminders in prison to make sure that he kept quiet. He was sent ten postcards, five from Kuala Lumpur and five from Hong Kong, with the simple message, 'Silence is golden'.

Less than a year after Jalil's murder, Carrian crashed with debts of HK$8 billion. It was soon obvious that the company had been built on bank loans. It became Hong Kong's largest and most expensive fraud case. George Tan's trial dragged on for fourteen years, during which time he had a heart attack and a stroke. It cost taxpayers HK$100 million. In 1996 he pleaded guilty to a US$238 million fraud and was jailed for three years. By the time the sixty-three-year-old was released he was seriously ill and taken straight from the custodial ward to a private hospital.

Jalil Ibrahim's life was not the only one lost over Carrian. Six months after Jalil's murder, John Wimbush, a senior partner at

Carrian's solicitors, Deacons, was found at the bottom of a swimming pool. He had a concrete manhole cover around his neck. Wimbush's death was ruled suicide. Months later, a Malaysian journalist investigating the story was killed. His body was found hanging from a tree in a banana grove.

As far as the courts are concerned, Jalil's murder is solved. But it is not for MacKillop. He has left both the force and Hong Kong, but he won't consider the case shut until the third person in room 609 has been identified. Fifteen years after Jalil's murder, MacKillop remembers the investigation in detail. 'I don't believe Mak Foon Than acted alone,' he says. 'I don't think he would have been able to keep a man of Jalil's knowledge and intelligence drinking cups of coffee while there was an important meeting going on at the Hilton.'

'I think there was someone else in the room, someone who was probably known to Jalil and I suspect a fairly senior official,' he says. 'We don't know what was being discussed in room 609 that afternoon, but it must have been very, very important, more important than what was going on at the Hilton, which was important in itself.'

MacKillop stops and runs through a checklist on his fingers of the evidence pointing to a third person: the room service deliveries, the briefcase the bell boy saw. And, he adds, the hotel staff said the door was locked from the inside on the night of 18 July, at a time when Mak was known to be out—a parking ticket with his fingerprints on it was proof of that.

'That person was fairly senior,' MacKillop muses. 'He has not been identified or arrested yet, so as far as I'm concerned, the case isn't solved, not to my satisfaction. At some point someone may talk, open up and tell the truth. I've got no doubt Mak was a murderer, but I don't think he acted alone.'

Wong Brothers: Loan Shark Empire

Wong Kwai-fun has been described by many as an evil man. He had one aim in life, to make money, and he didn't care what he did to get it. By the time he turned thirty, he was presiding over a loan shark empire that controlled more than half of Hong Kong's high-interest money-lending. He ruled by intimidation, and those foolish enough to think his threats empty soon learned the error of their ways.

Poverty helped shape this cunning bully. His parents had nothing to their name when he was born in 1956; they were hawkers and lived in a grim, dilapidated housing estate in Sham Shui Po, the district north of Tsim Sha Tsui. The couple worked from morning to night but made barely enough to survive, and life became even tougher as the family grew. Wong Kwai-fun was the eldest of five and although they were dirt poor, his three brothers and his sister were firmly bonded by sibling loyalty. It was on this bedrock of family trust that the loan shark operation was built.

In his early twenties, greed lured Wong into a forgery syndicate and he was jailed for making fake identity cards. His two-year sentence gave him plenty of time to weigh up his options. By the time he left prison in 1984 he had decided it was foolish to waste his time on petty crime. He was prepared to take bigger risks. Only money stood between Wong Kwai-fun and his dreams of power.

Most Hong Kong tycoons have achieved wealth through property, so Wong decided to try his hand. When he heard of a new housing development being built above a Mass Transit Railway station he wanted a piece of the action. Demand far exceeded supply so the government developed a ballot system to give everyone an equal chance. This prevented Wong from simply buying dozens of flats. The public ballot system gave all would-be homeowners an equal chance, but to circumvent the problem, he paid hundreds of people to submit application forms. From his stack of entries, all under different names, he drew twenty winners. He sold the flats immediately at a huge profit.

Wong must have had his tongue firmly planted in his cheek when he named his loan shark business Gentle Wealth. There was nothing gentle about the operation; if debtors didn't meet their repayments he would send someone around to let them know it hadn't gone unnoticed. He gave his family key positions in the company. His sister, Sui-fong, became the bookkeeper, and Wong Kwai-wing, only a year younger than him, was the chief debt collector.

Wong Kwai-fun wanted to make sure Gentle Wealth gave the appearance of a legitimate operation. Decked out in sharp suits and adorned with Rolex watches and mobile phones, his employees looked nothing like the common thugs they really were. But leaning against each desk in Gentle Wealth's Tsim Sha Tsui offices was a baseball bat.

Wong began by giving small loans—between HK$500 and HK$1,000—to labourers, and it was not long before he had businessmen knocking at his door. They were usually looking for quick cash to expand their businesses and Wong made sure they paid for it. He charged high interest rates, in the range of 400 to 500 per cent, and sometimes as high as 1,000 per cent. Many borrowers soon found themselves in a vicious cycle of debt. If the loans were not repaid, Wong would take possession of property and remortgage it with the bank. If a flat was worth HK$1.2 million, he would have it revalued at HK$1.8 million, which he would use as collateral. For their part, the banks would take a few thousand dollars under the table. More than one would come to regret their greed and end up in court.

Within a couple of years, Gentle Wealth had established a respectable front, with seven licensed money-lending shops, but the real business was run through another network of unlicensed premises. Wong Kwai-fun built up an impressive portfolio of debtors. The more people he had on his books, the bigger his network of control, and he used them all against each other. No fewer than 850 civil servants, 250 of whom were police officers, owed him money. Immigration officials were pressured into helping track debtors, telephone company staff were forced to give access to unlisted telephone numbers, and bank clerks were squeezed for confidential information.

Gentle Wealth's success lay in the terror that it instilled in its debtors. In many ways Hong Kong is a small town and for someone indebted to the likes of Wong Kwai-fun, it must have felt claustrophobic. There were few avenues of escape for those who could not meet their repayments, and police linked six suicides to the intimidation tactics of Gentle Wealth's not-so-gentle debt collectors. They would stop at nothing, from obscene telephone calls to having debtors beaten to within an inch of their life—and sometimes even that was not enough.

Wong Kwai-fun's activities were no secret to the police, who had a team dedicated to busting his operation. It was not easy. The loan shark king had spies in every sphere of Hong Kong life and his police contacts were especially good. One of his most useful informants was an officer named Tse Kwok-fu. At 1.9 metres, Tse was tall for a Chinese man, and his unusual height earned him the nickname Tarzan. Tse would pass on information about police raids to Wong Kwai-fun's brother, Kwai-nam. The inspector in charge of the loan shark case was Norrie MacKillop, who had an unshakeable faith in his team and refused to believe that an officer under him could betray him to the enemy. When one of his men, Bob Yule, mentioned his suspicions, he refused even to entertain them.

The entire team received threatening telephone calls from Wong's men. Typically the caller would say: 'Who do you think you're messing around with? You're out of your depth.' During a police raid one officer decided to take the direct approach and asked Wong Kwai-fun why he didn't simply retire since he had obviously already made a fortune. The loan shark responded: 'I can't—I've got 150 people under me. I must feed them.'

But his concern for his employees' welfare ceased when they fell into the same category as his creditors; they were treated the same way as anyone else who owed him money. His brother's right-hand man was to find that out the hard way. When forty-three-year-old Chong Kai-tak found himself unable to repay his HK$750,000 loan, he pleaded with Wong Kwai-fun for a chance to sort out his affairs. But the loan shark was not interested in his excuses. He ordered two of his men to beat Chong up.

The attack left Chong shaken and battered. Having worked for the company for two years, he knew that if he didn't repay his debt immediately Wong Kwai-fun's men would only become rougher. Fearing for his life, he fled Hong Kong and took a plane to South Africa, the furthest place he could think of from the Wong brothers. In the Transkei he hoped to begin a new life.

Wong Kwai-fun was furious. He was unused to being cheated and was determined that Chong Kai-tak should pay. Chong may have escaped, but his family was still in Hong Kong and Wong decided to hold them responsible. The loan shark king never did any of the dirty work himself—he farmed that out to a handful of thugs. Cheung Yu-cheung, a debt collector, was given the task of telling Chong's brother, Kai-ming, that he had incurred the debt.

Cheung did as he was told, telling the sibling that Gentle Wealth pursued a 'communist policy' and that Chong's whole family would be responsible for the troubles he had run away from. Chong Kai-ming, a factory owner, refused to pay the debt, and Wong's thugs moved on to a second round of threats. They spray-painted obscene slogans on the walls outside his flat and filled the lock of his front door with superglue.

The stunts may seem like little more than childish pranks, but there was no doubting the message behind them. When Chong Kai-ming refused to bow to the pressure, Wong Kwai-fun saw little alternative but to progress to the next level of intimidation. He gave Chong Kai-ming's address and car registration number to the debt collector and told him to turn up the pressure. The debt collector had links with the Sun Yee On triads and arranged for three Sun Yee On men to beat up Chong Kai-ming. It was standard procedure. The attack would be enough to let the victim know that Wong meant business, but not enough to do serious damage.

On 23 January 1987, the three triads waited in the multi-storey car park near Chong Kai-ming's apartment. It was early evening and they checked the registration number of each car as it entered. They spotted Chong as soon as he drove in and watched as he parked his car. He was walking towards the stairwell when the men pounced. The attack was frenzied; they beat him severely and hit him over the head with a metal pipe. Within a minute it was over and they fled. A neighbour found Chong Kai-ming a few minutes later and he was rushed to hospital. But the blows to his head had caused serious damage and he died three days later.

Wong Kwai-fun was becoming increasingly audacious. There was even a rumour that when the Police Commissioner ordered a special investigation into the loan shark empire, Wong Kwai-fun had a contract put out on the commissioner himself. Chong Kai-ming's death put pressure on the police to put an end to Wong Kwai-fun's business, but despite careful planning, their raids consistently failed.

In August 1988, Chief Inspector Ray Pierce took over the investigation. The team needed a fresh perspective and he was open to suggestions about how to tackle the case. Bob Yule, who had been on the team from the start, was convinced that there was a spy among them. He insisted that nothing could be achieved until the leak was plugged.

The next time they swooped on Gentle Wealth's offices, the police squeezed Wong's employees, demanding to know who warned them about the raids. Two men cracked and admitted they had been getting inside information. They said they didn't know the officer's real name, they only knew him as 'Code Seventy-seven'.

Discovering the identity of 'Seventy-seven' was a process of elimination. Ray Pierce drew up a list of suspects and deliberately fed each one false information, then he sat back and waited. Pierce was not surprised when 'Tarzan' Tse jumped at the bait. In 1990 Tse was jailed, and Wong Kwai-fun had lost his best spy.

Confident that his next move would come as a surprise, Ray Pierce prepared for a massive raid. In January 1989 his men, backed by a large support team, descended on twenty homes and offices linked to Wong Kwai-fun. Police seized dozens of boxes of documents. It would take investigators weeks to sift through the information and analyze it, but it was their first step towards convicting Wong. The loan shark king, thirteen female employees, and a handful of musclemen were arrested. Wong was charged with conspiracy to furnish false evidence to banks to raise HK$20 million. It was an unexpected family gathering for the Wong clan—two of Wong Kwai-fun's brothers, Kwai-wing and Kwai-nam, and his sister, Siu-fong, were also charged.

In the end Wong Kwai-fun was the only one to be sentenced. Wong Kwai-wing broke from the tightly knit family and fled to Taiwan, where he was safely out of the reach of the police (Hong Kong has no extradition treaty with Taiwan). There was insufficient evidence against Wong Kwai-nam, and Wong Kwai-fun made sure that his sister was not jailed. As the eldest sibling and head of the family business, he took the blame for her and had his lawyers propose a plea bargain that guaranteed her release.

Wong Kwai-fun was sentenced to four years but did not see prison as a necessary end to his empire, nor did he intend to spend his time idly. His first step was to begin plotting to ensure that the trial swung in his favour. Loan sharking had taught him much about manipulation and he saw no reason why he should not use the same tactics to secure his release. He drew up a list of people who could be coaxed into speaking in his defence and another list of those who he expected would speak against him. He would arrange to have this latter group discredited. He was confident that all he need do was give the lists to his brother and his wishes would be met. During one of his brother's regular prison visits, Wong slipped him the lists. But the plan went wrong when a prison guard spotted the papers and confiscated them.

Less than two years after sentencing, Wong Kwai-fun was back in the dock. This time he was charged with organizing the fatal attack on Chong Kai-ming. He pleaded not guilty, then claimed that the HK$750,000 loan to Chong Kai-tak had nothing to do with him. As for the papers he was caught passing to his brother, he said they were lists of people who were trying to blackmail him. The jury did not believe his story and found him guilty. Before the judge handed down a twelve-year sentence on top of the one he was already serving, he described Wong Kwai-fun as a 'man of violence and a menace to society'.

Wong Kwai-fun, used to getting his way, refused to believe that he would have to serve his time. His brother, Wong Kwai-nam, took on the task of securing his release and wasted no effort in appealing to everyone he thought might be able to help. In Hong Kong he petitioned the Governor, legislators, the Attorney-General, and the Police Commissioner. He flew to London and told his story to Members of Parliament and gave interviews to British television and tabloids. He even appealed to the Queen. Despite the ruckus, no one was willing to sympathize with his cause.

While his brother was singing his praises, Wong Kwai-fun was doing what he did best—loan sharking. With so many civil servants indebted to him, there were always useful people he could call on for favours. With the help of a few corrupt prison officers, he managed to run his business from behind bars. His activities did not go unnoticed. It seemed the only way to stop Wong Kwai-fun was to isolate him, so in July 1992 he was transferred from Stanley Prison to the maximum security wing of Sui Lam Psychiatric Centre.

By early 1994, Wong Kwai-nam had spent three years campaigning for his brother's release. Frustrated that his hundreds of appeals and petitions had come to nothing, he took a more direct approach. On 23 March, he waited outside the Legislative Council for the Attorney-General, Jeremy Matthews. As soon as he saw him, Wong Kwai-nam stepped out of the crowd and threw a bottle of black ink at him. As far as Wong Kwai-nam was concerned, the stunt was successful. The

Attorney-General was saturated through to his underpants, and Wong Kwai-nam was again in the spotlight. He took the opportunity to highlight what he saw as the unfair treatment of his brother by both the police and the Legal Department.

Wong Kwai-nam moved on to more aggressive tactics when the Privy Council in London refused Wong Kwai-fun's appeal. He began a hate mail campaign. Worried that his own handwriting would be recognized, he advertised for a clerk. One of the applicants was a young graduate from the Mainland. Wong Kwai-nam knew she was keen to get the job and he told her part of her duties would be to act as Wong Kwai-fun's 'girlfriend'. To make sure that she remained loyal, he told her to strip and photographed her naked. The pictures of the twenty-four-year-old could be used to blackmail her if she ever dared turn against him. Wong Kwai-nam showed the snaps to his brother for his approval and asked the girl to have a flower tattooed on her stomach as a sign of fidelity. She then became one of Wong's' regular prison visitors. Confident that she could be trusted, Wong Kwai-nam told her to copy threatening letters that he had prepared. The poison-pen letters, written in her hand, were sent to prominent civil servants, lawyers, and judges.

Wong Kwai-nam threatened everyone. He even sent a vicious letter to the Chief Secretary, Anson Chan. To prove that his threats were not empty, he arranged to have Chan's cousin beaten. Five days after the attack, he sent another letter warning that Anson Chan and her family would be in serious danger if she did not order a reinvestigation of Wong Kwai-fun's case.

Clearly, the legal fraternity had not impressed the Wongs. Wong Kwai-fun's barrister, Gerard McCoy, received one of the letters threatening his family. McCoy was taking no risks and he put his wife and two young children on a plane to New Zealand. Barrister Kevin Egan, who had successfully prosecuted the loan shark, was another obvious target. His office was bombarded with up to 100 telephone calls a day from strangers who had been paged with messages to call the barrister's office. Wong Kwai-nam also sent letters to dozens of solicitors warning them against dealing with Egan. The Attorney-General received a threatening letter, as did the Correctional Services Commissioner and two judges.

The police gave the hate mail campaign top priority and soon traced the letters back to a company run by Wong Kwai-nam. In 1996 his case went to court and he was sentenced to three years and eight months for criminal intimidation. No sooner had he been sentenced than further charges were made against him over other threatening letters. The threats against Anson Chan were serious, but the government was reluctant to let the Chief Secretary testify. To save her from having to take the witness stand, a plea bargain was reached. Wong Kwai-nam agreed to plead guilty to sending threatening letters to Anson Chan and Kevin Egan, and in return, eight other charges, including a blackmail case against Wong Kwai-nam and Wong Kwai-fun, were dropped. The deal added an extra fourteen months to Wong Kwai-nam's sentence, for a total of four years and ten months behind bars. He was not disappointed. He saw the plea bargain as a victory, and he had managed to get the charges against his elder brother dropped. In mid-1997, Wong Kwai-wing, who had been on the run for seven years, returned to Hong Kong and was arrested. He joined his brothers in jail.

Wong Kwai-fun was the first to be released. He wasted no time slipping into his old lifestyle, and was wearing an expensive dinner suit when his limousine picked him up from the prison gates in March 1999. He had everything to be happy about; not only was he free, but the family business assets had multiplied while he was behind bars. Wong Kwai-fun was a very wealthy man.

Triad Gangsters

The triads are the Chinese equivalent of the Mafia. They infiltrate everyday life for much of Hong Kong, from restaurant owners to minibus drivers.

Triads often recruit youths from school or housing estate playgrounds. These teens form gangs and bully non-gang members, but they are not fully fledged triads. Many of them drift away after a few years but others stay on, join a street gang, and are initiated as a 'forty-nine'. These make up the bulk of the triads, the rank-and-file members who are the criminal workforce. The forty-nines quickly learn the criminal ropes of gambling, prostitution, and extortion. They also fight to protect the gang's interests and may be called on to act as hit men. Their pay depends on their success and their boss takes a commission from their salaries. Most triads remain forty-nines all their life, but some are promoted to the rank of officials. Officials, known as Red Poles, are responsible for running their gang's criminal activities, leaving the dirty work to the forty-nines.

Andley Chan, nicknamed the 'Tiger of Wan Chai', was a Red Pole. His gang's chief criminal enterprise was extortion from restaurants. Triads make contacts in the food industry, so that they can exploit the vulnerability of restaurants. They may, for example, control the daily delivery of fresh foods, such as vegetables and noodles. If the delivery is delayed, the menu will be limited and the restaurant's reputation will suffer. Faced with this kind of power, it is not surprising that businesses bow to triad pressure.

Today's triad societies are descended from secret associations that were formed in China hundreds of years ago as a means of self-preservation. There are four main triad groups in Hong Kong, including the 14K, the Wo On Lok, and the Sun Yee On. After the Communist defeat of the Kuomintang in China in 1949, a 14K leader fled southern China (the Communists had put a price on his head) and escaped to Hong Kong. The 14K quickly became one of the largest triad groups in Hong Kong, and by 1955 it had a membership of 80,000 in Hong Kong and elsewhere in South-East Asia.

Although triad societies have come a long way from their honourable beginnings and are now without exception criminal forces, they have held onto many of the traditional rituals. Secret ceremonies serve to keep the gangs united; the rituals are steeped in the Oriental occult science of numerology, in which numbers and patterns of numbers take on an esoteric symbolism.

The most important ritual is the initiation ceremony, which involves payment of a joining fee, symbolic face-washing, reading poems of fidelity and allegiance, and, crucially, a list of thirty-six oaths. If any of the oaths are broken, the punishment is death.

7

An Eye for an Eye: the Tiger of Wan Chai

Andley Chan Yiu-hing had the looks and charisma of a film star. Tall and well-built, he wore the trendiest shell suits and the latest trainers, and his hair was always perfectly groomed. He had a reputation to maintain. His vicious temper had earned him the nickname 'Tiger of Wan Chai', the number one triad in the district that inspired Richard Mason's novel 'The World of Suzie Wong'. Aside from a smattering of 'girlie' bars, the brothels had all but gone, replaced by gleaming tower blocks. The Sun Yee On triads ruled Wan Chai and Chan was 'top dog', the leader.

Chan was a natural leader, exuding confidence and thriving on attention, but success had not come easily. He began, as many triad underlings do, with valet parking. Only those with serious money can afford cars in Hong Kong, the land of the luxury automobile. Parking the cars of the rich has its perks, one of which is illegal road racing. While the owner is tucked away out of sight in a fancy restaurant, a young triad might be at the wheel of his car. Chan graduated from valet parking and climbed up the underworld ladder to become a Red Pole, one of the highest ranking officials in the Sun Yee On, overseeing the extortion rackets in Wan Chai. Yet he never lost his taste for the thrills of the road and a high-speed chase. From such humble beginnings came one of Hong Kong's most infamous triads, a big fish in a small pond. But this fish splashed about enough for the ripples to be felt in neighbouring pools.

For all Chan's handsome looks and careful grooming, he was still a fighter. He had been brought up on the street and could more than hold his own. But as he rose through the ranks of the Sun Yee On, he had less cause to turn to violence. Such was his position and reputation that intimidation would usually suffice. There were times, however, when a show of force and physical violence was called for. The last big street battle Chan summoned was in April 1991. Collecting protection money was his bread-and-butter business, so when he heard of a new seafood restaurant opening in Wan Chai he was keen to make sure the Sun Yee On were its 'protectors'. But he had competition. A rival triad group, the Wo Hop To, also had an eye on the restaurant. Chan was determined not to let another gang move in on his patch. It was time, he decided, to show just who was the boss.

One phone call was all it took to summon more than 100 followers to Wan Chai's main thoroughfare, Lockhart Road, at around 10pm one evening. Emerging from the shadows, they stepped out into the street, some pulled up on motorbikes, others jumped out of vans. Eyes darted warily but their expressions gave away nothing. Jaws set rigid, no one spoke. Within five minutes the street was packed. Chan's men chewed drinking straws and their rivals wore baseball caps—it was the only way of distinguishing the two gangs. The air was thick with tension as they jostled on the street, sizing each other up. Words were exchanged at the centre of the tense knot and then someone shouted out—a war cry. Knives were pulled from under jackets, flicked open, and thrust forward. The fighting was frenzied as the men lashed out. Chan's fighters, straws still tightly clenched between their teeth, began to take the upper hand. Others, arriving late, threw themselves into the mêlée. It had been just five minutes, but already men were doubled up, blood welling from deep gashes in their arms. Then, seized by a collective panic, the Wo Hop To turned and fled. Chan and his men chased them down the street, jeering. It was another victory for Chan, reasserting his position as the kingpin of Wan Chai.

Protection money made up the bulk of Chan's business interests, but he was a man with his fingers in a number of pies. The one that most fascinated him was the film industry. With his looks and triad clout, he blended easily into the fabric of the beautiful people—starlets, singers, and directors. Chan's stake in the world of the big screen was nothing new. Triads have always been on the set of Hong Kong's film industry, doing what they do best: demanding protection money. As film-making is expensive, a delay of only a few days can be enough to force a movie to be abandoned. Triads therefore demand a fee to ensure that props are looked after, that film does not go missing, and that stars are taken care of. Hong Kong triads are extremely territorial. Anything that happens on their patch is their business. They may demand 'rent' for filming on their territory and foreign movie-makers are not exempt. In 1973, the Sun Yee On disrupted the filming of a scene for *The Man with the Golden Gun* outside the topless bar Bottoms Up in Tsim Sha Tsui. This was Sun Yee On territory, but it never occurred to the producers that they would need triad permission to film on the street.

Such actions were fairly petty and had as much to do with face as with territorial gain. But as the film industry took off in the late 1980s, the triads wanted a bigger piece of the action. They wanted a say not just in the making of films but in their distribution as well. And with the triads came intimidation.

Heavy-handed techniques were used to persuade stars to accept scripts. One actress was raped for not agreeing to the terms of a triad producer, and an actor was reputedly forced to eat his own excrement. Amy Yip, a glamorous actress, was asked by a triad producer to bare all for the camera. Her refusal was not well accepted and she had to seek police protection.

Anger at triad influence in the film industry reached a crescendo in 1991 and early the next year actors, actresses, and directors took their grievances onto the street. The protest was not the last time triads in the film world would make headlines that year. A few months later a minor incident would have fatal repercussions for Chan, unleashing a chain of events that would lead to his murder.

Anita Mui, an actress and singer, was so popular in the early 1990s that she topped the local charts and could do more or less as she pleased. 'Established' in an industry infiltrated by the triads invariably meant links with one of the gangs. Mui was closely associated with the Sun Yee On, though, of course, she denies this. In May 1992, she threw a birthday party for her assistant, Carrie Chan. She booked out Take One karaoke bar and it was almost open house for anyone in the entertainment industry. The beautiful mingled with the powerful, with strings of young girls hanging on the arms of unlikely heroes. In a private booth, surrounded by close friends and admirers, Mui held court.

Among the guests was Wong Long-wai, a film producer. His biggest achievement, *Legend of the Chow Brothers*, tells the story of 1960s drug lords who fled to China. The film had been successful and made him known among the triads, particularly the 14K, with whom he was closely associated. Wong was in a confident mood—he had drunk a little and the compliments were flowing. Spotting Mui on the karaoke stage, he greeted her with a warm familiarity and jokingly requested a song. The singer gave him a cold stare, slowly looking him up and down, and turned her back on him. It was a huge public put-down, a massive loss of face for Wong: the hostess of the party had deliberately snubbed him. Without pausing for thought, the producer spun Mui around and slapped her across the face. All eyes were on Wong. For a few seconds no one moved. Then life flooded back into the room as Mui turned on her heels. Friends rushed to console her. Wong wisely exited.

In Hong Kong such scenes are not shrugged off lightly. Wong must have been expecting a rebuff of some sort for slapping Mui, but he was not prepared for what was to come. Two days later, he was leaving a Chiu Chow (Chao Zhou) restaurant on Jaffe Road in Wan Chai, Sun Yee On territory. Jaffe Road runs parallel to Lockhart Road and is much quieter. Only a few restaurants were still open and a video store was preparing to close. Wong had eaten well and was chatting with a friend as they ambled along the almost deserted street. As the pair walked past an old tenement building, two men jumped out from the shadows. Each held a large chopper and in one fluid motion they attacked Wong. The producer raised his arms to cover his face as the blades whipped across his forearms. Wong's friend caught a few turns of the knives, but he escaped relatively lightly. The attack was clearly directed at Wong. He shouted out as he tried to fend off the blows and dropped to his knees, cowering beneath his attackers with his arms raised over his head. The assault was over in less than two minutes and the attackers escaped into the night.

Wong lay slumped in a pool of blood as his friend ran for help. He was rushed to the Baptist Hospital. His injuries were serious but treatable. With care and rest he would recover and in hospital his wounds did begin to heal. Naturally, for a man in his condition the doctors kept a close eye on him, but they could not have known what was to come. It was Wong's second night in hospital, the lights were dimmed, and the ward quiet. Three nurses on night duty talked in hushed voices as their patients rested. Suddenly there was the sound of gunfire. The nurses rushing from the end of the ward slammed on the main lights to find Wong crumpled in his bed. The gunman had fled from this second assault on Wong's life in as many days. The nurses managed to stop the bleeding and called desperately for support, but this new attack proved too much and Wong died two days later.

Days after the producer's death, Chan was arrested in Macau and brought back to Hong Kong for questioning. He and a friend, Wong Sik-ming, were charged with the Wan Chai attack on the producer. Chan was granted bail on condition he surrender his travel documents and report to the police twice a week. A court date was set for early 1994, but Chan would never appear before a jury. In the triad underworld justice is dispensed on the streets.

It was business as usual for Chan. He was preoccupied with the development of a prestigious shopping centre, Times Square, which was being built in the neighbouring district of Causeway Bay. The centre would attract many restaurants, which meant more protection money for Chan and his men. He used standard triad tactics: he sent three or four of his men to each restaurant while it was under construction. The young thugs would intimidate the workmen into handing over the name and phone number of the restaurateur. A meeting would then be arranged with the owner at a nearby restaurant. The men were familiar with the law and were careful not to incriminate themselves. Rarely would they say they represented the Sun Yee On. They would merely explain they were a local gang and needed to discuss security arrangements. Chan usually avoided businesses owned by foreigners because they could often spell trouble. But he was getting greedy. He targeted all the restaurants in the complex, regardless of ownership.

Wan Chai detectives knew the state of play. In an effort to preempt the Sun Yee On, they contacted all the restaurant owners and advised them to report any extortion attempts. Local Chinese invariably pay up without a fuss—protection money is an expected overhead and is often even tabled into operational costs. However, foreigners do not accept extortion as easily. Chan made a mistake when he sent his men to talk to the manager of a new Mexican restaurant in late 1993. Heinz Grabner had no intention of turning over 10 per cent of the rent—HK$30,000—every month to the triads. He stalled for time, saying he needed to talk to his business partners, but instead went straight to the police. When Chan's men returned to the restaurant, Grabner was ready to talk business. A couple of Wan Chai detectives posing as his partners sat in on the meeting. When they had enough evidence to prove extortion, they arrested the pair. Further raids over the next two days led to the arrest of twenty triads, including Chan and his younger brother.

The arrests were a serious loss of face for Chan and he was angry that he had been tricked by a Westerner. The press were not about to let the story rest. The most popular weekly Chinese magazine, *Next*, carried a piece about Chan and his valet parking days. Chan was furious and retaliated immediately. He could be revered and respected, but he was not prepared to be the subject of tabloid exposés. He sent a handful of his men, armed with metal bars, to the magazine's office. They smashed the plate glass lobby window and devastated the reception area. The magazine's publisher, Jimmy Lai, would also feel the brunt of Chan's rage. Later that night, a Molotov cocktail was thrown into the driveway of his house. The attacks began a month of violence, but it was Chan himself who would be the next target.

The Macau Grand Prix was held two weeks later, on 21 November. It is the highlight of the motor racing calendar in Asia. Chan was not about to miss the weekend of fun, especially as he was signed up for one of the races. A close friend and film producer, Simon Lo, had sponsored his car. Chan and his friend, Wong Sik-ming, flouted their bail regulations to attend the event in Macau. The day began well and Chan was in a confident mood. In the pit with the smell of engines he was in his element. On the track he pushed himself, daring his nerves on the corners and pushing flat out through the stretches. He came in second, but the glory was short-lived. Officials quickly disqualified his car because of illegal modifications. The ruling did not stop him celebrating and he joined his two mechanics and the producer Lo in the bar at the New World Emperor Hotel.

Every hotel in Macau that weekend was booked out, and the bars and restaurants were packed with journalists, car enthusiasts, and tourists. Chan and his friends talked, drank, and laughed at each other's karaoke attempts. At 3am, they decided to call it a night. Lo stayed behind to settle the bill; he would catch up with the others in the car park. Walking through the hotel foyer, an antique caught Lo's attention. He was admiring the piece when he heard a series of loud bangs. 'Firecrackers,' he thought to himself, assuming the noise to be part of the Grand Prix celebrations. As he opened the door leading to the car park a British woman rushed past him into the lobby screaming, blood gushing from her leg. In the car park, Chan was slumped over the steering wheel of his van. He had been hit in the left temple and chest and died almost immediately. Both his mechanics had been hit as well. One survived but the other died in hospital a few days later.

The injured British woman, Gillian Martin, was among the few witnesses. She had been walking through the car park when she saw three hit men pull up on motorbikes in front of Chan's van. One of the gunmen fired at Chan's head from point blank range. The glass blew out from the passenger side window. Chan managed to start the engine, but the van only rolled a few feet before rocking to a halt. The gunman then turned on Gillian. Terrified, she tried to pretend that nothing was happening, that she was merely hurrying to catch a cab. He lowered his gun, aimed at her shin, and fired—another triad warning.

It was a professional hit and the gunmen fled the scene on their motorcycles, leaving almost no evidence. An enquiry was launched into the killing, but it produced more complaints than murder leads. The Macau police criticized the Hong Kong police's investigative methods as 'British', formal, and laborious. They felt the force's insistence on doing everything by the book was interfering with the investigation. The Hong Kong side refused to be drawn into the dispute, although they did say language differences hampered the investigation. No one was ever charged with Chan's murder or that of his mechanic, but there was little doubt that those responsible were avenging the film producer's murder a year earlier. Wong Long-wai's links with the 14K made them the most likely assassins.

Chan's funeral was huge. Outside the funeral home the reporters jostled for space and photographers climbed bamboo scaffolding for a better vantage point. The press were on the lookout for Chan's girlfriend, TV presenter Chan Miu-ying. She had been warned that the funeral would be mayhem and instead went straight to the crematorium. The police did not miss the opportunity for large-scale surveillance—at few other times would they witness such a large gathering of triads. They frisked the more than 200 mourners as they entered the funeral home. Most were Sun Yee On triads dressed in uniform black suits and dark sunglasses. The entertainment world kept its distance. Celebrities were too wise to the ways of the press to make an appearance, instead paying their respects more anonymously with floral tributes. Wreaths and scrolls bearing condolences covered the walls inside the home. The centrepiece was a table with large framed photos of Chan and the mechanic. Next to the portraits were joss-sticks, fruit, and other offerings. In Cantonese, the number three (*sam*) sounds like the word for 'life', and three cans of Heineken and three packets of Marlboro cigarettes, each with three cigarettes half pulled out, were displayed on the table. The mourners followed the black hearse, which drove the bodies to the crematorium. Following tradition, paper money and paper models of luxury items—mobile phones, ships, and cars—were burnt. The Chinese believe that the money and goods will pass through to the afterlife with the deceased. The money can be used to bribe the gods and the other goods are for enjoyment. Several paper cars were burnt to make sure that Chan was not without wheels on the 'other side'.

There was talk of infighting among the Sun Yee On as members fought to take Chan's place. Fearing that the gang's rivals, the Wo Hop To and the 14K, would exploit the confusion and challenge the Sun Yee On's position in Wan Chai, the police stepped up patrols after the funeral. The rumoured gang wars turned out to be nothing more than hype. Chan's younger brother, Yui-hong, moved in to fill the Tiger's shoes. The Sun Yee On kept their niche in Wan Chai, but Yui-hong lacked his brother's strength of character. He was cold where Chan was charismatic, hesitant where the 'Tiger' was headstrong.

Despite Chan's death, the court hearing into the murder of the film director went ahead. Chan had escaped sentencing, but the charges still stood against his right-hand man and close friend Wong Sik-ming. Six months after Chan's funeral, Wong Sik-ming stood before the court accused of being a Sun Yee On member and of wounding the film director. But prosecutors could not prove he was a triad. As for the wounding charge, the judge ruled there was not enough evidence: Wong Long-wai's friend had only glimpsed the assailants in poor light.

Journalists surrounded Sik-ming as he left court. As he struggled through the crowd reporters asked him to comment on the case. It seemed he would remain silent, but as a car drove up to collect him he turned and addressed the press pack: 'All I can say is that the Tiger of Wan Chai gave us, the *lo fu tsai* [the little tigers], his blessing.' But what of the bigger picture? Reporters demanded to know the significance of the killings. Wong gave a wry smile: 'It's beyond my control. One death followed another.'

Not long after Chan's death, Hong Kong's film industry slumped. The decline was partly due to the triads pushing their weight around. Taiwanese investors who had boosted the local market had had enough of their interference, and turned their attention to their own fledgling film industry. Similarly, triad-weary mainland film-makers decided to try their hand at their own movies. But the triads cannot take all the blame. Hollywood blockbusters were stealing the limelight and Hong Kong's action movies simply could not compete. The kung-fu action movie, for which Hong Kong was famous, had been overdone, leaving the plots stale and contrived.

As money bled from the industry the triads lost interest, although they did not abandon it altogether, and Chan would not be easily forgotten. Less than a year after his murder, a film was released about his life—*Tragic Fantasy: The Tiger of Wan Chai*. True to the spirit of the Tiger, the making of the film was as controversial as the movie itself. Stephen Lo, who had been drinking with Chan minutes before his assassination, produced the movie. After its release, both the director and a stunt man took Lo to court, complaining he had threatened them into doing the film. Chan's real-life girlfriend, Miu-ying, played herself, but in the film version she is with Chan when he is gunned down. This poetic licence added to the drama of a man who, at thirty-two, died young enough to earn mythic cult status. It was the film's glorification of Chan and his triad ways that riled the police. Ironically, Chan's character was played by actor Simon Yam, the brother of a senior anti-triad officer.

Cigarette Smugglers: Death of the Informant

Tommy Chui's bloated and battered body was found floating off Singapore's Clifford Pier on 1 April 1995. It bore all the hallmarks of a triad killing. His head was swathed in thick packing tape, wrapped tightly around his nose and mouth. His body had been placed in two nylon bags and weighed down with diving weights.

Clearly the killers had wanted the body to be identified. The victim's wallet, complete with cash and membership cards to prestigious Singapore clubs, had been left inside the bags. As investigators and triad experts pieced together the clues, it seemed the killers had deliberately left a message: informants would not be tolerated. Chui's murder came less than a month before he was due to give evidence in Hong Kong against some of his former business partners.

Tommy Chui had been a very wealthy man. At the time of his death, his personal fortune was estimated at HK$100 million and he and his family were preparing to move into their dream home, a HK$60 million mansion in one of Singapore's most prestigious districts. Chui moved among Singapore's social elite—he was a member of the Swiss Club and a select shooting club—and held a Canadian passport. He had more than his parents could ever have dreamed of. They had fled Shanghai in the 1950s to begin a new life in Hong Kong. But life was difficult and there were few luxuries in the Chui household. However, after leaving school early and working as a seaman and then a salesman, Chui had helped found a business that led to his fortune.

In 1986 Tommy was a sales manager for Towyn, a firm exporting imported wines and Winston and Salem cigarettes. Through the introduction of friends, he met Hung Wing-wah, a businessman and entrepreneur who ran a trading firm exporting electrical appliances, herbal medicines, wine, and cigarettes to Taiwan. Tommy Chui was hoping to strike a deal with Hung to help him sell cigarettes in Taiwan, but Hung had a better idea: why not set up a company together?

Giant Island Limited (GIL) was formed later that year to sell cigarettes to China and Taiwan, and Tommy Chui left Towyn to work for the new company. Chui held a 12.5 per cent stake in the firm and Hung owned 67.5 per cent. The remainder was split between two of Hung's partners: Chen Ying-jen, whom Hung had met in Taiwan, and Chong Tsoi-jun, one of Hung's employees. Hung trusted Chong implicitly, largely because he came from Fujian (Fukkien), Hung's home province in China. Hung made Chong responsible for the day-to-day running of GIL and the company accounts.

The business was not a legitimate enterprise. China has the world's largest cigarette market—one-third of the world's cigarettes are smoked on the Mainland. In order to protect its market, China levelled a 1 per cent quota on foreign cigarettes and imposed import taxes as high as 400 per cent. This created a thriving black market and made the smuggling of foreign cigarettes into China highly lucrative.

The most popular cigarettes on the Mainland are 555, the brand GIL focused on because it promised the biggest profits. GIL obtained its cigarettes from British American Tobacco (BAT), but everything had to be under the table, as BAT had no joint venture with China. Without a formal agreement to sell its cigarettes, the only way that BAT could get its huge supply into the Mainland was through the 'back door'. GIL needed a steady supply of 555 and the demand was met thanks to a corrupt BAT Commercial Director. He was Shanghainese, so it fell to Chui to do the talking. Their home city provided an immediate link.

Chui proposed the idea and they came to an agreement: the director would be given HK$150 for every box (containing 250 cartons) of cigarettes sold to GIL. For his part, the director would have to guarantee supply, thus flouting the strict export regulations. He did. Each month he received HK$1.5 million in bribes. Chui would meet the director at the Country Club, a private club on the south side of Hong Kong Island, to give him the money. Over dinner he would hand over a manila envelope stuffed with HK$1,000 notes. This arrangement went on for a couple of years and by the time the director emigrated to Canada in 1988, he had pocketed HK$45 million in bribes.

The next Commercial Director was from Fujian province. As Hung was from the same region, he made the initial contact. A similar arrangement was struck and Hung took over the role of paying the monthly bribes. Although GIL reduced the commission to HK$50 per box, the demand was far greater. GIL ordered an average 40,000 boxes a month, giving about HK$2 million in bribes a month to the BAT director.

Jerry Lui was in line to be BAT's next Commercial Director. Eager to ensure his share of the lucrative trade, he approached GIL before his appointment was even confirmed. He wanted HK$2 million in advance and a further HK$3 million if he were made commercial director. It was a bold move, but GIL accepted it. The bribes continued much as before, although rather than handing over the money in cash, it was paid directly into Jerry Lui's Union Bank of Switzerland account.

During its first year, GIL found it was losing considerable business having to wait a full day for an export permit from the Duties Commodities Administration. A solution was provided by a customs officer, Henfrey Tin. He had grown up on a housing estate controlled by the Wo On Lok triads and had climbed the ranks to become one of the group's senior members. Tin called Chui saying he might be able to help, and suggested they meet for dinner. During the meal he said he could ensure GIL's export permits were processed quickly and pass on information about the operations of similar traders. Chui agreed on the spot and gave Tin the HK$20,000 he asked for in cash.

The delays with the export permits disappeared overnight. Tin also introduced Chui to customs officers, known as 'chicken biscuits', attached to the various warehouses. Chui gave each officer a one-off bribe. The 'greeting gifts' of about HK$5,000 were enough to ensure GIL was given preferential treatment.

There were several ways to smuggle the cigarettes. The 'vegetable base method' involved collecting cigarettes from a bonded warehouse and taking them to the cargo handling area. There they were loaded into containers. Eleven ships travelled regularly between Hong Kong and the southern Taiwan port of Kaohsiung (Gaoxiong). GIL had shares in six ships, each of which would carry a container stuffed with 4,000 boxes of cigarettes. Space would be left at the front for a façade of legitimate goods, such as television stands. Midway through the journey, the ship would stop and the cigarettes would be transferred to fishing boats. The boxes were wrapped in plastic and covered with a layer of ice to hide them. All the connections were in place and the business ran smoothly. The bribes were considerable, but the profits were even bigger. Hung made more than HK$15 million a month smuggling 132,000 boxes of cigarettes.

It was not until late 1989 that GIL hit its first major obstacle. A rival cigarette exporter, Wing Lee, which was controlled by the Sun Yee On triads, wanted a piece of the action. Henfrey Tin, the customs officer who had sped up the export permit process, offered to help. Drawing on his Wo On Lok triad contacts, he said he would talk to the rival group. Accompanied by one of his triad brothers, Tin met two Sun Yee On triads at GIL's offices. The Sun Yee On introduced themselves using their nicknames, one known as 'Bearded Lam', the other as 'Dark Cow'. Intimidation is the rule among triads and Tin made the first move. He told the Sun Yee On that 200 Wo On Lok triads were waiting outside, prepared for any trouble. Bearded Lam drew a gun and pointed it at Tin. The threat was nothing more than an attempt to show Tin that they were also serious, and there was no violence. They arranged to meet again.

The next meeting was at the Trotting Club. Tommy Chui, Hung, and two Wo On Lok triads met the rival firm's bosses. After long talks, they agreed that Tin would be responsible for shipping cigarettes from Hong Kong to Taiwan and that the Sun Yee On would get a share of the profits. The deal was a success for GIL and Tin was rewarded for his help by becoming GIL's protector. His triad background and experience as a customs officer made him a useful person to have on board. Rather than being given a salary, Tin was sold about 3,500 boxes of 555 cigarettes a month at a cheap rate. Two years later, this figure was doubled and Tin set up his own company to sell his supply, at a huge profit.

While it was in GIL's interests to have Tin's protection, his new appointment with them meant they had lost their chief contact in the Customs Department. The preferential treatment they had received dwindled and in mid-1990, GIL was facing new problems. Again, it was Tin who saw a solution. He had a good contact in Hong Kong's anti-corruption watchdog. Alex Tsui was the deputy director of the Independent Commission Against Corruption (ICAC). Henfrey Tin had met him twenty years earlier when they were both working as customs officers. They were drawn together by a shared love of kick-boxing and they kept in touch after Tsui left the department.

Tsui's friendship with Tin had not gone unnoticed by the ICAC. In 1986, he was asked about his relationship with Tin after the triad had been charged in connection with an armed robbery. Tsui insisted his friendship with Tin had involved a 'serious error of judgement' and said he had nothing to do with Tin any more. That was not the case, however, and rather than sever his links with Tin, Tsui soon broadened them.

Tin introduced Chui to the ICAC officer. It was an informal meeting at a restaurant, but Chui kept his guard up. He knew the ICAC was investigating cigarette smuggling and he chose his words carefully. After some small talk, he told Tsui about the Sun Yee On's attempt to take over their business. Tsui said he could make a formal complaint, but Chui said not to bother, it was too 'troublesome'. It seemed Chui was throwing Tsui hints about the Sun Yee On in an attempt to draw attention away from GIL.

After that first tentative meeting, Chui soon realized he could trust Tsui and by the early 1990s they had formed a close friendship. Chui even developed an interest in kick-boxing and took lessons from Tsui for a while. Following kick-boxing etiquette, Chui called Tsui 'master'.

Tsui knew the ICAC would not approve if they discovered he was still in touch with Tin. Rather than wait to be caught out, he decided to approach the matter head on and asked for permission to see his friend again. His request was granted on the condition that he opened an informant's file on the triad. Tsui opened a file codenamed 'Florence'; it was little more than a formality and Tsui recorded very little in it.

While GIL's business flourished, so did the Boxing Association. In March 1992, Hung became the association's chairman, with Chui, Tsui, and Tin on the executive committee. Tsui's position in the ICAC lent the sport a new respectability, and boxing matches attracted the recognition of senior government officials. Meanwhile, GIL's operations continued to rake in millions of dollars each month, but their activities were not as secret as they had hoped. The ICAC was gathering intelligence reports on the main players. Tommy Chui began to feel uncomfortable. GIL's ships were registered in his name and he was worried that if anything were to go wrong, he would take the rap. He decided it was time to get out.

In April 1993, Chui and his family left Hong Kong to settle in Singapore. He sold his shares in GIL to Hung and Chong and set up his own cigarette business in the Lion City. The move did not spell the clear break that he had hoped for. Two months after leaving, Tsui and Tin flew to Singapore to see him. They knew the ICAC's investigations were closing in on GIL and were eager to make sure Chui kept quiet.

In June, the ICAC questioned Henfrey Tin about a HK$1 million loan he had made to a senior triad. The triad was alleged to have organized the killing of a bar hostess a year earlier. Tin admitted he had lent the money, but insisted this was not unusual—he said he often lent money to friends. The ICAC had nothing to charge him with and let him go.

Immediately after the questioning, Tin rushed to the Macau ferry terminal to keep an appointment with Tsui. Tin later said the trip was to discuss Boxing Association business—a tournament was in jeopardy and they needed to settle the matter. He insisted he had not spoken to Tsui about his interview with the ICAC. Regardless, the trip to Macau spelt the end of the road for Alex Tsui. The Boxing Association and the visits to Macau and Singapore had done nothing to ease the ICAC's concern and they had since learnt about a loan Tsui had made to Tin eight years earlier. In November 1992, Alex Tsui was sacked from the ICAC.

He immediately disputed his dismissal, claiming it was a political manoeuvre by a colonial and racist body. His allegations threw doubt on the integrity of Hong Kong's corruption watchdog. The press and public demanded to know the reason for his sacking, but the ICAC insisted it was confidential. The ICAC Commissioner, Bertrand de Speville, had told only a select few, including the Governor Chris Patten and the Executive Council. After a month of intense publicity and widespread rumours, legislators demanded an investigation into the sacking. It took a ten-month inquiry to settle the matter and the final verdict backed the ICAC's decision.

Meanwhile, the Anti-Smuggling Task Force swooped on a timber yard in the New Territories on 15 March 1994. It was one of the force's biggest busts. They found twelve million of GIL's cigarettes hidden in wooden pallets and aluminium doors. Tin and Hung were arrested but released after two days of questioning. Hung felt it too dangerous to stay in Hong Kong and decided to quit while he was ahead. He flew to Switzerland where he cleaned out his bank account, taking the US$150 million he had accumulated from the smuggling operation. He then fled to Vancouver, Canada, where he now owns a dozen luxury apartments.

Tin was going nowhere. His release was on condition he surrender his travel documents for six months. In October 1994, this was extended for a further three months. He called Chui in Singapore and warned him that ICAC investigators would probably visit him. 'Just remember, you are not obliged to tell them anything,' he warned. The phone call was the beginning of a series of attempts to persuade Chui to keep quiet.

Less than two weeks later, Tsui was in Singapore and met Chui for dinner. Much of the meal was spent discussing Tsui's dismissal. He was still angry and said he planned to sue the ICAC. Then he asked whether the ICAC had been in touch with Chui. 'Tommy, you have the right to say nothing to the ICAC. Better to put away a grudge than to bear it,' Tsui said, and warned Chui not to return to Hong Kong. Two weeks later, on 14 April, Henfrey Tin called Chui again and reminded him that he was not obliged to say anything. It was too late; Chui had already made up his mind and that same day he gave his first of three statements to the ICAC. Tommy Chui had turned informant.

When Henfrey Tin and Alex Tsui learned that Chui was talking to the ICAC, they stepped up the pressure to keep him quiet. 'Forgive and forget,' he was told. Later that month, a friend visited Chui and warned him that a plan was being hatched to have him killed. He advised him to go to Canada until the matter had blown over.

Tin called Chui again on 28 April. Fearing, correctly, that the phone was tapped, he told Chui not to mention his name. His threats were barely veiled and his conversation was peppered with references to Chui's health. In a desperate bid to keep Chui quiet, Tin arranged to meet Chui's brother-in-law, Wong Ka-lik. He drove him to the Windsor Sauna in Wan Chai. It was an ideal meeting place for Tin. Not only did he have shares in the place, but the towel-only dress code ensured that Wong was not bugged. After their sauna, they moved into the rest room, where Tin got down to serious business.

'You are the only one who can rescue me," Tin told him. He explained that Chui was to be a witness against Hung for bribing BAT staff. He said although Chui was a good friend, Hung was his patron, and he did not want to let him down. He said he would pay Wong's airfare to Singapore if he agreed to go there and persuade Chui to retract his statement.

Wong took the next flight to Singapore, but Chui was not prepared to bow to the pressure. Instead of revoking his statement, he took his brother-in-law to the ICAC. Wong was advised to return to Hong Kong and to tell Tin he had done as he was told; Chui was considering his request. A couple of days after his return to Hong Kong, Tin met Wong at the Excelsior Hotel. Tin tried to persuade him to go to Singapore again, but Wong said he had the flu and backed out.

The Windsor Sauna in Wan Chai has a sister sauna in Singapore; both are by run by the Wo On Lok triads. The Singapore sauna was headed by Teddy To and Ringo Wong. This would be the base camp for Tin's next step in his plan to keep Chui quiet. It seemed the only way to make sure Chui said nothing was to silence him for good. Tin sent two men to Singapore to begin preparations for Chui's abduction and murder. The men were Cheng Wui-you, known as Ah Tee, and Lee Yiu-man, known as Ah Man. Following Tin's instructions, they got in touch with Teddy To at the Windsor Sauna and asked him to help them find a place to stay in Singapore.

Teddy To arranged for Ringo Wong to look after Cheng and Lee. Wong had gone to school with one of them in Hong Kong and they had an immediate rapport. He let them stay at a flat usually reserved for sauna staff. A couple of weeks later, Tin sent three more men to Singapore: Cheng Hing, Wong Kwong-kai, and Cheung Wai-ming. Like the first two men, they had strong links with the Wo On Lok triads.

It soon became clear that their mission would take time, so after a month they rented a flat. The apartment—55A Paterson Road—was under Ringo Wong's name and the five men spent most of their time together. They followed Chui and began devising a plan to abduct him. Their free time was divided between the sauna, discos, and restaurants. Aside from Lee Yiu-man, who was staying with his Singaporean girlfriend, the men lived at the Paterson Road flat. During the months that followed, the men returned to Hong Kong regularly to report on the progress of the plot to abduct Chui.

In December 1994, Tin was re-arrested, along with his trusted Fujian partner, Chong, who was responsible for the day-to-day running of GIL, and a former customs officer, Yeung. The ICAC knew about Tin's threats to Chui and were concerned for his safety. At the court hearing they tried to keep his identity secret by referring to him as 'Witness X', but few doubted who had informed the ICAC. Tin was handed a string of charges, the chief one being the acceptance of a HK$20,000 bribe in 1988 while he was a customs officer. He was also charged with plotting to smuggle cigarettes, conspiring to offer bribes to customs officers, conspiring to defraud the government, and attempting to pervert the course of justice. Chong, for his part, was charged with plotting to offer bribes to tobacco company executives and government officials, as well as trying to influence Tommy Chui. Yeung was charged with plotting to smuggle cigarettes and defrauding the government.

As soon as the magistrate granted the three men bail, prosecutor Kevin Zervos jumped to his feet and insisted this was unwise. Tin had already tried to persuade Chui not to give evidence and Zervos was worried that the threats against the prime witness might become more serious. The magistrate dismissed these fears, but after private discussions in chambers he conceded that Tin, Chong, and Yeung posed a risk to Chui and ruled that the three should be re-arrested. A date was set for a preliminary hearing—26 April 1995—and Chui was to take the witness stand a few weeks after that.

Meanwhile, in Singapore, the plan to abduct Chui was well underway. Tin's henchmen had been keeping a close eye on Chui. Every morning he drove to his office in his Porsche and parked in a nearby multi-storey car park. After several hours in the office, he usually broke for a long lunch and often played golf before heading home in the early evening. He was always alone in the morning, so the men decided this would be the easiest time to grab him.

They stole a maroon Honda Accord and a silver Accord and switched the number plates in preparation for the abduction. Two weeks later, in the early hours of 29 March, they stole a car from Shenton Way car park, where Chui parked his Porsche, and transferred the car's magnetic car park pass card to the Honda. After a few hours' rest, the men drove to the car park to wait for Chui.

He arrived at 10.30am, as usual. The men rammed the side of his Porsche and pulled him from his car. They knocked him unconscious and bundled him into the boot of the Honda. One of the men drove the Porsche and the others jumped in the Honda. Flustered by the attack and unfamiliar with the car park, the men drove up to the fifth deck before speeding away.

Chui was taken to a secret location, where he was bound, gagged, and beaten. The beating was severe, but it was not what killed him. Packing tape had been stuck over his nose and mouth and he died of asphyxiation. The men slept much of that afternoon in their flat, then they packed their bags and spent the evening at the Windsor Sauna. The following day all five returned to Hong Kong. As far as they were concerned, their job was done and they could return to their regular lives. But this was not to be.

The evening of Chui's murder, his wife, Florence, was opening a boutique. When her husband failed to turn up for the launch party, she called the police. Two days later, on the morning of 1 April, Chui's body was found floating in Singapore Harbour. It had been placed in two canvas bags of a kind commonly found in Hong Kong, but not Singapore. The first bag was padlocked around his neck. His body was weighed down with nineteen kilograms of lead diving weights. Three diving belts had been strapped to his body, with four, five, and six lead weights respectively.

A triad expert called to the scene said that the number of blocks of lead was part of a triad ritual. The first two sets of weights, he said, represented the five lakes and four seas of triad brotherhood. This suggested that Chui was a triad member. The six weights on the other belt indicated that Chui had breached the sixth of the triads' thirty-six oaths, which forbids triads from doing anything that might lead to the arrest of another triad. By acting as an informant, Chui had signed his own death warrant.

Hours after Chui's body was discovered, the Porsche and the Honda were found in another multi-storey car park. The Porsche had a long white scratch mark down the left side. The Honda, which had been abandoned one floor below, had blood stains in the boot. Three keys were found on the ground next to the Honda—the keys to Chui's Porsche and house. It was no accident that they had been left behind. The triad expert insisted that their positioning represented the Chinese symbol for triad in general and the Wo On Lok triads in particular. Chui's killers had left behind their calling card.

Hong Kong papers reported the news of Chui's murder amidst widespread speculation about a Hong Kong link. Unnerved by the high-profile coverage, the gang fled Hong Kong to Thailand. Less than a week later they were on the run in mainland China.

They travelled to Kunming, Beijing, Shenzhen, Guangzhou, Guilin, and Hainan. Along the way they met up with their wives and girlfriends, who brought them supplies, including Hong Kong magazines and newspapers that they could not get on the Mainland.

The men were eventually caught and brought to justice in Hong Kong, but not before the GIL executives had been tried. Yeung was released after a four-day court battle. But Tin did not get off so easily. In August 1995, he faced a new charge of conspiracy to pervert the course of justice by trying to prevent Chui from giving evidence, and several weeks later he was further accused of plotting to murder Chui.

The prosecution dropped the other charges and proceeded only with the allegations relating to Chui. His case was set for trial in November, and attention turned to Chong.

A day before he was due in court, Chong slipped in the shower and seriously injured his back. That was far from his only piece of bad luck. The next day, the magistrate stopped the proceedings, saying there was not enough evidence against him, but just as it looked as though he might get off, Kevin Zervos brought up a new charge. Chong was accused of a HK$60 million tax fraud, the biggest in Hong Kong's history. He was granted bail and went straight to hospital to be treated for his back injury. Some months later, he was re-arrested and charged with plotting to offer a HK$20 million bribe to a tobacco executive. Days before the trial was due, Chong committed suicide by jumping from his twenty-sixth-floor home in Mid-Levels.

The next courtroom drama erupted when a defence barrister complained that vital evidence was being withheld. Chui's brother-in-law said that there was no truth to the allegations he had made about Tin and he wanted to withdraw his comments, but the defence were not informed about his retraction. The judge said he regretted the slip-up but insisted on continuing the trial. After days of talks behind closed doors a deal was struck. Tin pleaded guilty to plotting to pervert the course of justice by trying to stop Chui giving evidence. In return, the charge of conspiracy to murder was dropped, and Tin was sentenced to five-and-a-half years.

By the time Cheung Wai-ming and Wong Kwong-kai reached court, charged with plotting to murder Chui, the most substantial evidence the prosecution had was gathered while they were in a holding cell. The pair had shared a cell with a man called Leung Sze-lai, who was on a murder charge. He told the ICAC that he had overheard the two discuss the cigarette smuggling operation and said that Cheung had admitted to killing the prime witness, Chui.

The conversation was crucial to the case and much of the trial centred on its validity. Many laughed at what they saw as a desperate attempt to cobble together evidence. The defence introduced a former prisoner, who claimed Leung had told him that he had made up the conversation in the hope of shortening his own sentence. Leung denied fabricating the conversation.

The defence, led by Australian barrister Kevin Egan, was struggling but still feisty. When the prosecution provided sketches of the abduction scene, scribbled in a magazine found in the Paterson Road apartment, Egan tried to undermine the prosecution's witness. Eric Lye, an eminent architect, had confirmed under oath that the sketches were of the car park where Chui was abducted. The Australian barrister asked the architect to study a sketch he had drawn and to comment on it.

The architect studied Egan's drawing and told the court that he thought it was a sketch of a road junction with trees and a building at the bottom. Kevin Egan had been hoping for such a response and, with pleasure, informed the jury that the sketch was not one of a street, but in fact a plan of the court. This was not to be Egan's only wisecrack in the face of a flagging defence. Chief Inspector Ip Pau-fuk also came in the line of fire. When the triad expert had finished giving his evidence on triad rituals and the symbolism surrounding Chui's murder, Egan asked him: 'Do you by any chance have a part-time job as a storyteller at children's parties?'

There was not enough evidence to convict Wong Kwong-kai, but Cheung was not as lucky. On 4 November 1998, he was sentenced to twenty-seven years for plotting to kill Chui.

'It is difficult to think of a more planned, calculated, cold-blooded approach to the removal of a person who was to give evidence in a trial in Hong Kong,' the judge said as he sentenced Cheung. Only then were the jury told that this was not Cheung's first murder conviction. In 1988, he had been jailed for the vicious triad chopping of a restaurant owner in Scotland.

Kidnappings

Chinese society has always favoured males. The birth of a boy is announced with much fanfare. A boy represents security for parents who know they will be able to rely on their son to look after them in old age. But baby girls do not receive the same welcome. They are often seen as just another mouth to feed and are a poor investment, since when they marry they leave their own family. China's one-child policy has exacerbated this misogynist view and in some areas extreme devotion to young sons has given rise to a phenomenon known as 'little emperors'.

These young boys are so spoilt that sociologists are seriously concerned about what these demanding children will grow up into. In 1995, a ten-year-old threw a tantrum when he came home from school to find his mother had failed to cook his favourite dumplings. He did not simply sulk, he cut off her head and threw it out of the window.

There is no one-child policy in Hong Kong, but boys are undoubtedly the favoured sex. During his twelve years with the Hong Kong Police, Chief Inspector Steve Vickers worked on sixteen kidnappings. Without exception, all of the victims were male. Women simply do not command the same value as men.

9

Tycoon Teddy: A Watched Man

Like many billionaires, Teddy and Nina Wang lived in a mansion on the Peak. A most impressive address. Yet in a neighbourhood containing some of the world's most expensive real estate, their home stood out not because of its luxury but because of its state of decline. The untended grounds had grown thick with weeds and the house needed a complete makeover. But to Teddy Wang this meant nothing; he was loath to waste money on something he saw as superficial. Instead, he poured his energy into Hong Kong's favourite pursuit—making money, and more money.

In his teens Wang had followed his father into the chemical business, traipsing around the countryside convincing farmers of the benefits of fertilizers. His early wanderings gave him a good idea of the development potential of the New Territories, helping him make wise decisions when he turned to property investment. Wang kept full control of the company, ChinaChem, and always made deals personally. His life was ordered and he made an art of punctuality. But despite his hands-on approach, he kept a low profile. He stayed away from the social circuit, preferring more solitary pastimes such as reading and horse riding.

Children might have created a little chaos in the Wang household, but he and his wife, Nina, had none. She was the demure Chinese wife, or *tai tai,* that a man in his position expected. Nina Wang was petite. She stood just 1.50 m tall and her tiny frame shook when she laughed. But she did not laugh often. It was not that she was unhappy—she loved her husband and could not imagine life without him. She was simply undemonstrative. Her quiet modesty might have misled some into thinking her dreary. Far from it: her reticence masked eccentricities, foibles that wealth not only permits but nurtures. She

Teddy Wang

loved dogs and treated them as though they were her children. When Wang asked her if she wanted to join the company, she agreed only on the condition that she be allowed to bring her German shepherd. Wang permitted his wife some indulgences. But for himself, even a chauffeur was an unnecessary expense. He drove to and from work himself in a white Mercedes. So it was on Tuesday, 12 April 1983 that the Wangs left for the office at 8.30am, as always. If he had not been so punctual, he might have saved himself a lot of trouble.

Wang had barely shifted out of second gear when a truck blocking the road forced him to stop. Two men jumped out of the van and walked towards the car. Wang wound down his window and with a wave of his hand signalled for the truck to move out of the way. Ignoring Wang, the elder of the two, a muscular man in his late twenties, pointed a gun through the open window. The other man yanked open the passenger door, grabbed Nina Wang's arm, and held a knife against the pale flesh of her wrist. Their demand was simple: 'We don't want to kill you, we just want money. Get out of the car.'

The man with the knife shoved Nina Wang into the back seat. She caught a glimpse of her husband from the rear window as he was pushed into the truck. A hand grabbed her shoulder and twisted her around. She was given a pair of glasses and told to put them on. The lenses had been covered with paper and the world went black when she did as she was told. She heard the car start up and then one of the men spoke to her. Their organization wanted money and if she did not cooperate her husband would die. She was not to call the police and if she left Hong Kong, they would find her. His instructions were simple: to open an account with the Overseas Trust Bank (OTB) and wait for further directions. Nina Wang was shaking when they let her out of the car, but she did as she was told.

Meanwhile, Teddy Wang had been gagged, blindfolded, and bound with wire. He was shoved in a refrigerator in the back of the truck. When the truck stopped half an hour later, Wang suspected he was on Kowloon side. He had felt the truck pull up at a pay toll, go through the cross-harbour tunnel, and then stop at another pay toll. He was right, he had been driven to Hung Hom, an area of high-rises and warehouses north-east of Tsim Sha Tsui. The refrigerator was taken out of the truck and pushed a short distance. Wang was lifted out, his hands and feet secured with iron chains, and pushed onto a bed. The men returned a few hours later. They called each other by numbers rather than names. The one called 'Eighteen' took off his blindfold. Wang blinked as his eyes grew accustomed to the light. He was in a dimly lit room. There were no faces to be seen: the men had covered their heads with plastic bags. He was handed a piece of paper and ordered to recite the words on it into a tape recorder. When the recording was made, Eighteen took out a camera. The flash momentarily blinded Wang, then he was plunged into darkness as the blindfold was slapped back on.

Nina saw the photograph that afternoon. The image of her husband bound in chains staring into the camera must have been a shocking and haunting sight. Earlier, a man who referred to himself only as '1188' had called and told her to go to the public toilets in Beaconsfield House in Central district. There was a parcel for her in the fourth cubicle. She did as she was told. The package contained the picture of Wang, the keys to the Mercedes, and a cassette. She listened to the tape at home. She was to deposit US$11 million into the OTB account within four days and put an advertisement in the *Sing Tao Yat Pao* newspaper giving the account number. She sat alone for a long time wondering what to do. When she eventually stood up, it was to call the police. Despite the kidnappers' warnings, she felt she had no alternative. Detectives advised her not to give in to the kidnappers'

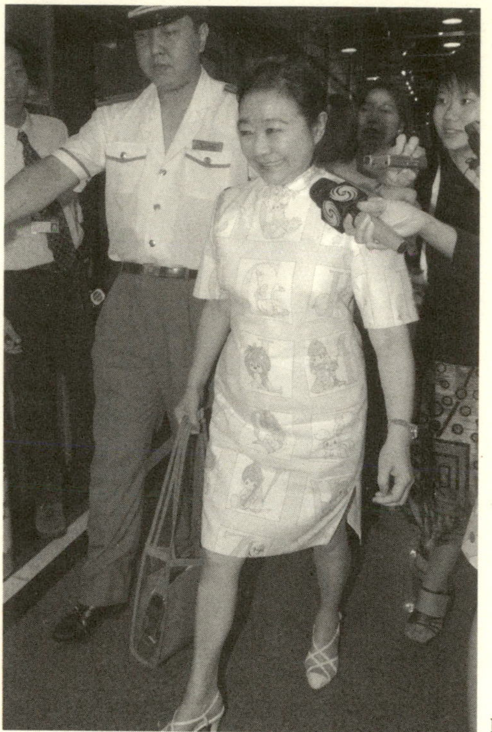

Nina Wang

demands, advice she was initially prepared to accept. The phone rang a few hours later. It was 1188 to say he would call her at her office in the morning.

Nina was in the office early. She arranged the newspaper advertisement and then waited for the call. It did not come until mid-afternoon. She told 1188 she was having trouble raising the money and asked if other arrangements could be made. 'Definitely not,' came his curt reply, and he hung up. He called again an hour later and warned her not to play games. Afraid that something might happen to Wang if she stalled, she ignored the advice of the police and deposited the US$11 million ransom in the new account. Two days later, on Friday, 15 April, 1188 called to check that she had followed his instructions, and the next day he rang again and gave her directions to another package. This time the parcel was hidden in a fire hose on a staircase. Along with two recent photographs of Wang, still in chains, were another cassette and typewritten instructions. She was to go directly to the bank and transfer the ransom money to an account in Taipei.

The next days proved a nightmare as she waited for word from the kidnappers. Nina spent an agonizing weekend next to the phone, hoping and praying that her husband would be returned safely. The call from 1188 came on Monday. The money had been cleared by the bank in Taipei. With no proof that her husband was alive, Nina nearly broke down on the phone, so much so that 1188 tried to calm her, reassuring her that her husband was fine. He called the next day to tell her the money was being transferred to another account and that Wang would be freed before Friday, 22 April.

On the Wednesday, Wang heard something heavy being moved into the room. Still blindfolded and disorientated, he struggled to sit up. The wire around his hands and feet had cut and blistered his skin in places, but otherwise he was fine. He felt the chains around his ankles being released and he was gagged with a piece of packing tape. A voice close to his ear startled him. He was told to get up and hands guided him into a metal trunk. The box was pushed a short distance on a trolley and then loaded onto a van. When he heard the hum of the engine, he struggled to free his hands. Without too much difficulty, he eased them out of the wire. He was tempted to remove the blindfold but decided against it. He did not want to give them any reason to kill him.

Half an hour later the van came to a halt. Wang's heart was pounding. He did not know if he was about to be killed or freed. The trunk was opened and he was helped out. Surely if he were to be killed the men would treat him more roughly, he thought. Hands guided him out of the van and he was made to sit on the kerb. He was told to count to 500 and then take off his blindfold. Instead he tore it off as soon as he heard the van drive away. He saw the van; it was white and in the back window there was a sticker with the words 'Jesus loves you'. He tried to read the registration number and just caught the first two letters, CU, before his captors turned a corner.

Wang continued staring at the bend in the road long after the van had disappeared. He had no idea where he was. There were no street signs or even lamp posts and a thick wall of trees and shrubs lined either side of the road. It was hot and within a few minutes he could feel beads of sweat trickling down his back. The sound of an approaching car snapped him out of his trance-like state. As it turned the corner he saw it was a taxi. It felt strange to do something as normal as hailing a cab after eight days in chains. The driver did not raise an eyebrow at his dishevelled appearance, but did give him a suspicious look when he floundered over a destination. 'Just drive,' Wang told him. Five minutes later they reached the main road and Wang realized he was in Sha Tin, a sprawling commercial and residential area in the New Territories. His brother-in-law ran a clinic in the district, so Wang directed the cab there. He was still dazed when he walked into the clinic and before he even began to explain what had happened he grabbed the phone and called his wife.

Nina Wang wept when she saw her husband. She wanted to lock the door and have him all to herself, afraid that he might disappear again. But the police were keen to speak to him first. He was still shaken and spoke in a lively, animated way that was out of character. Nina Wang watched her husband in silence, her face streaked with tears. The police were not pleased that she had paid the ransom, but they had been afraid to intervene in case a change of plan made the kidnappers edgy, putting Wang's life at risk. Wang, too, was far from impressed that his wife had handed the money over, but he would deal with that later. His first concern was to recover the ransom by helping the police with information. The number plate and the window sticker gave them a strong lead.

Finally the police left, leaving Wang to wash off eight days of captivity and get some rest. Far from looking for comfort, however, Wang instead berated Nina for paying the ransom. Even though her actions may have saved his life, she had been foolish to go against the advice of the police. Wang's fears appeared well founded; by giving in to the kidnappers' demands on this occasion, they had made themselves vulnerable to similar attempts in the future. But his displeasure ran much deeper than simply anger at his wife for not following police advice. For a man with a fortune of many billions of dollars, US$11 million is a relatively small amount. Yet Wang saw the money as wasted, despite the fact that it may have saved his life. Teddy Wang has been bluntly described by some as a miser. Had the kidnapping changed his view of spending money on personal security, he might still be alive today.

Given his immense wealth, Teddy Wang's attitude to money can be difficult to understand, but put in the context of his Hong Kong peers he is not an anomaly. Hong Kong's tycoons are among the richest people on earth, but most came from very impoverished backgrounds. They left the Mainland with nothing, fleeing the Japanese, the Cultural

Revolution, or poverty. The city's most famous tycoon, Li Ka-shing, arrived in Hong Kong penniless. On his father's deathbed, the younger Li had vowed to make enough money to support his mother and siblings. He made more than he could ever have dreamed of, but he never forgot what it was to have nothing. In a land of Rolex and Gucci timepieces, Li wears a cheap, plastic watch because, he says, it tells the time just as well. Sally Au, heiress to the Tiger Balm fortune, is another person notorious throughout Hong Kong as a bargain hunter.

Concerned for Wang's safety, the police gave him twenty-four-hour protection at home. Four men, working split shifts, stood guard outside the Wang house for several weeks after the kidnapping. Teddy Wang was not asked to pay for this round-the-clock protection; it came courtesy of the Hong Kong taxpayer. However, as there were no cafés in this exclusive area, it was naturally assumed that he would at least provide meals for the men. But Wong simply disliked spending money, and not once in all the weeks of free security did he arrange to have food brought out. The meanness of this is all the more striking when one realizes that, thanks to police intelligence, Wang managed to recover 78 per cent of the ransom.

The police called him the day after his release, with news that they had made a breakthrough in the case. They had found the van in the car park of a housing estate in Sha Tin; it was registered in the name of Lo Siu-chung and had been bought on hire purchase with the countersignature of a Leung Yun-fuk.

The police spent the weekend trying to track down Lo. It was not until the following Monday that they got lucky. The Immigration Department had been put on alert and he was picked up when he tried to board a flight to Bangkok. Lo did not look like the kind of criminal who could mastermind the kidnapping of a tycoon, let alone launder the ransom money. He was twenty-eight and worked as a labourer at a container terminal. After a little rough police persuasion, he was willing to talk.

Lo told how his foreman at work had asked him if he wanted to become part of a gang planning a kidnapping. Lo was swayed by the money—his cut would be between HK$500,000 and HK$1 million. Only when he agreed was he introduced to the other gang members. He told police about Leung, with whom he had shared a flat in the run-up to the kidnapping. To Lo, who spent his life eking out an existence, Wang's wealth was beyond comprehension. As a child his parents considered him lucky to have been fed and when he began earning a meagre salary they expected him to hand over a good deal of it.

After the kidnapping Lo was given HK$50,000 and told he would get the rest in Bangkok. Never having had so much money, he immediately went out on a spending spree. The first thing he wanted was a designer watch, the kind of timepiece he could use to impress people. The Rolex he bought set him back HK$10,000 and the DuPont pen and lighter set he spotted in the same shop cost a few thousand dollars. He also spent HK$30,000 on prostitutes in the space of a few days. When Lo Siu-chung was picked up he only had HK$8,000 left. It was not much, but it was more than Leung Yun-fuk had.

Leung was arrested at Kai Tak Airport a few days after Lo, as he too tried to board a flight to Bangkok. He was a few years younger than Lo and came from a desperately poor family. Barely literate, he had left school at the age of twelve to begin work to help support his eleven younger siblings. Leung had accepted a paltry HK$20,000 for his part in the kidnapping. He had hoped it would buy him a better life, but instead it bought him a decade behind bars. Lo was also sentenced to ten years. Two other gang members were arrested and convicted in Hong Kong, but it proved more difficult to bring to justice the ones who had fled the territory.

The man who had orchestrated the laundering of the money in Taiwan was a Hong Kong resident, Yip Wing-tim. He was arrested in Taipei, and although he fought to be repatriated to Hong Kong, his requests were denied. The local police could do nothing, as there is no extradition treaty between Hong Kong and Taiwan. Under Taiwan's Nationalist Chinese law, Chinese suspects are allowed to be tried regardless of where their crime has been committed. Yip was thus tried in Taipei, where the courts are much tougher, and in 1984 was sentenced to death. But he had a reprieve a year later, when his sentence was commuted to fifteen years. It must have seemed a long time to a man who never saw any of the money. To him, Wang's millions were just numbers on a computer screen. He never received a cent.

Meanwhile, the mastermind was still at large. When he was eventually tracked down two years later, it was under bizarre circumstances. In August 1985, Thai police rescued a Hong Kong man named Chan Kam-chuen, who had been abducted by a gang of seven men and was being held for an HK$2.8 million ransom. The ransom was haggled down to HK$250,000, but when the gang went to pick up the money they fell into a police trap. As a matter of course, the

Thai police ran the name of the man they had rescued through the computer. They were shocked to see he was on an international wanted list for kidnapping. Chan fled to Thailand after Teddy's release in 1983. He lived there with his Thai wife outside Bangkok. But word got out that he had been involved in the kidnapping of a Hong Kong tycoon, and a Thai gang tried to do the same with him. Chan was made to stand trial in Hong Kong in 1986, but his case was delayed for years as the courts waited for the extradition of another gang member, Jenny Pao, from Florida.

Pao fought the extradition. The Tiananmen Square massacre in 1989 added fuel to her Miami lawyers' arguments. Hong Kong's return to China was just eight years away and if Beijing could run tanks over innocent students, there was no telling what it might do to a convicted criminal. Her lawyers argued that repatriating her to Hong Kong could mean a death sentence. While Pao was disputing her extradition, Chan was sitting in a prison cell awaiting a hearing. In late 1989, he was granted bail because it was thought that if he remained in prison he might overrun his eventual sentence.

Just months after Chan was freed on bail, Teddy Wang was kidnapped again. Chan was the first person to say that he had nothing to do with it. There were plenty of other criminals who knew of Wang's wealth. He was the thirteenth-richest person in Hong Kong, with a fortune of HK$7 billion. The 1983 kidnapping had done nothing to make him more careful, despite access to the security arm of his company. He refused to vary his lifestyle, preferring to stick steadfastly to an unwavering daily routine. He left the house at 8.30am every morning, drove his Mercedes to the office, and returned after his workout at the gym at exactly the same time.

Yet again, punctuality was Wang's downfall. When he left the Jockey Club on 10 April 1990, he had no idea that he was under observation. Nor did he realize he had been watched for the previous five months as the kidnappers studied his daily movements. Unbeknown to Wang, he was followed by a man on a motorcycle, who relayed the tycoon's progress to a gang of six waiting in two cars. When Wang reached a winding section of Peak Road, a car screeched in front of him and another pulled up behind. Sandwiched between the two he was forced to stop.

A man jumped out of one the cars and ran towards him with an axe. He smashed it against the window, which shattered on the second blow. The man, who wore leather gloves, pushed a hand through the window, quickly unlocked the door, and tried to pull Wang out, but the tycoon braced himself against the dashboard. Two more men appeared; one flicked open a knife and waved it in Wang's face, ordering him to get out.

They were much rougher and more efficient than the first kidnappers. In less than a minute, he was tied up in the back of the Mercedes. The man with the axe took the wheel, spun the car around, and sped back down the hill. The two other cars followed. Two men in the back with Wang gripped him firmly and pushed his head down by their feet. He was thrown against the front seat as the Mercedes hit another car and skidded. There was a blast of a horn, but they did not stop.

They drove past Aberdeen Harbour, a large fishing community on the south side of Hong Kong Island. Small, open-topped sampans shuttle visitors to and from large, floating seafood restaurants, among Hong Kong's most popular tourist destinations. The Mercedes sped past the tourist lights and drove across a bridge to Ap Lei Chau Island, the real heart of the fishing community. Here an oily tide splashes against the harbour wall, and the bricks are ingrained with the smell of seaweed, salt, and stale fish. A string of shops selling fishing nets, lanterns, and lines faces the sea. During the day, it is a colourful, noisy neighbourhood, but the street sleeps early, and at night it is quiet and deserted.

Wang was pulled out of the car and taken down a narrow lane. The Mercedes was pushed into the water, floating briefly before being swallowed by the sea. This time there would be no car keys returned to Nina Wang, no snapshots of her husband in captivity. In a small, roughly furnished room Wang was ordered to drink a glass of Coke. He refused but the man insisted. Wang must have guessed the drink was spiked and it would have been with a quiet terror that he felt his limbs go numb.

He tried to fight the drug and although remaining conscious, he could not move. It must have seemed as though he were watching someone else as the men tied him up and fastened an iron weight to the end of the rope. Four men carried him across the road and down the stairs set into the harbour wall. A sampan was waiting and the men struggled to get him aboard. The sampan slipped between fishing boats and out to sea, expertly negotiating the choppy water and riding the waves. After twenty minutes, just off Lamma Island, they drew up alongside a fishing boat. It was much like any other, the wood painted black and trimmed with dark green. Wang was hauled aboard and the fishing boat sailed to just within Chinese waters, where he was transferred to a bigger craft. The deck was a chaos of thick ropes and tangled nets. This was to be Wang's home for the next few days.

When her husband failed to return home after the gym, Nina Wang feared the worst. Wang lived according to the clock and a delay of half an hour meant something was wrong. She knew he would not alter his routine without telling her. Memories of the earlier kidnapping haunted her and she prayed it had not happened again. An hour after Wang was due home, Nina called the police. Their advice was the same as it had been in 1983: do not pay a ransom.

The ransom demand came the following day; inflation and greed had boosted the figure to an astonishing US$60 million. Two detectives and 300 officers were put on the case. One of the senior detectives was Chief Inspector Steve Vickers, the kind of man who might have been called an 'old China hand' a decade earlier, but who was too self-consciously modern for such a tag. Vickers was a kidnapping connoisseur. He had been called in on fifteen abductions and all the victims had been released safely. He was looking forward to another notch on his belt.

One of the key jobs for the police was to calm Nina Wang. They were afraid she would crack and pay the ransom. In addition, the press suspected something was amiss and were snooping around for information. An explanation was needed urgently and was found in a short-term solution. A ChinaChem executive stood up at a press conference to say that Teddy Wang had been injured in a riding accident. He had fallen off his horse and was in hospital. Reporters pressed for more information. Had he sustained head injuries or brain damage? Eager to end the discussion, the executive ended up saying Wang had both types of injuries, but then added unconvincingly that he would return to work within a week. Some Chinese papers speculated that Wang had been kidnapped, beaten, and freed—it was the beating that kept him in hospital. They could not have been further from the truth.

As Vickers had feared, Nina Wang could not handle the pressure. She crumbled beneath the kidnappers' demands and agreed to pay half the ransom. Vickers was furious, but there was little he could do; stopping the payment would have put Wang's life in danger. He and his team could only trace the money and hope to find Wang without scaring his captors. With a tap on Nina Wang's phone line, they had traced one of the kidnapper's calls to Guangdong province in southern

China, but knew this was most likely just a staging post. The money was probably destined for Taiwan.

When HK$260 million lands in a private account overnight, eyebrows are bound to be raised, and the half ransom that Nina Wang paid into the kidnapper's Taipei account did not go unnoticed. For months, the Taipei police had been investigating a money-laundering operation thought to be linked to arms smuggling from the Mainland. They immediately assumed the HK$260 million was connected to this case. The money was tracked down to a plush hotel in the capital, and when police raided they found sixteen fruit boxes stuffed with the ransom money in New Taiwan dollars and share certificates. Six people were arrested in the hotel immediately. In Hong Kong, another six were captured and eventually handed sentences of up to sixteen years.

Wang was never seen or heard of again, but one of the kidnappers told a court what had happened. On the third day of his capture, a Chinese navy ship had spotted the boat on which Wang was being held. The navy gave chase and, fearing that they would be caught, the kidnappers threw their victim overboard. Trussed up, drugged, exhausted, and attached to an iron weight, Wang stood little chance of survival.

Vickers had lost his first kidnap victim. It was a dent to his pride, but he did not feel responsible. If he had been able to run the investigation his way, he was convinced Wang would have lived.

Although no body was ever recovered, the police felt certain he was dead, as did everyone else, except Nina Wang. She has never given up hope, and just as Teddy Wang's death is ingrained as a Hong Kong story, so is Nina Wang's rise from the ashes.

At times she felt the darkness and grief would swallow her, but she held on. After two years, Nina Wang snapped out of her depression, cast aside her misery, and became a changed woman. Calling herself the 'Chairlady', she took over at the helm of ChinaChem. She was the only woman in a boardroom dominated by men, but she did not let that intimidate her. There were sighs of exasperation and knowing nods as people waited for her to slip up and lose the company millions. But under her careful management ChinaChem grew and diversified: biotechnology companies in California, factories in mainland China, and, of course, properties in Hong Kong—200 of them.

Nina Wang became the kind of woman she had been afraid even to approach before. She exuded confidence. Though close to sixty, she followed the latest trends, wore miniskirts, loved discos, and took her German shepherd everywhere. She also never let go of her dream that Wang was still alive.

In court there were rumours that in closed chambers she had reported receiving phone calls from her husband. As far as Nina Wang was concerned, her husband might walk back into her life at any moment. However, there is another, much less charitable reason for Nina's stubborn refusal to accept his death. According to Wang's will, drawn up in 1968, his entire estate was to go to his father. If Wang was not dead, of course, the will was invalid. Wang's father took Nina Wang to court and the case went on for months. When it eventually reached the Court of Appeal, the judge looked in horror at the papers. He could not believe the case had gone so far when the most obvious point had been overlooked: Wang had not been proven dead. Only when it was agreed, legally, that the tycoon had left this world could his will be acted upon. Nina's insistence that Wang was alive confused and delayed the matter further. In early 1999, she threw another spanner in the works. Almost a decade after his disappearance, she presented her lawyers with a sealed envelope, claiming it contained Wang's last will. It could only be opened, she said, if it were proved that he were dead.

And so Nina Wang remains the chairlady of ChinaChem. She grew, not through her husband's presence but through his absence, to become a canny, strong-minded businesswoman. But there is one quality she has held onto, a legacy of her relationship with Wang. Although she is the fifth-wealthiest woman in the world, she still loves a bargain, and can occasionally be spotted queuing on street corners to get cut-price theatre tickets.

10

A Botched Attempt: The Unlikely Victim

Lai Tak-sum was a gentle fourteen-year-old. The only child of doting parents, he could be trusted to go to school fifteen minutes after his parents had left for work and always be home in time for dinner. But he could not have been prepared for what would happen on 5 January 1982. As he left the shabby estate a man in his early twenties tapped him on the shoulder and said someone wanted to speak to him. Pointing at a green Datsun, he ushered the boy across the street.

The man opened the rear door and as Tak-sum went to look in, he gave him a rough shove, pushing him onto the back seat. 'Keep your head down,' barked another man in the driver's seat and the boy was thrown forward as the car suddenly accelerated. He did as he was told, but after five minutes he sneaked a look. 'Uncle Sang,' he cried, recognizing the driver.

'I said keep your head down,' Chau Suk-sang snapped and he shot an angry glance at his partner, Chan Siu-ming. They drove to the south-east of the New Territories, what must have been a tortuous half-hour journey for the boy. He knew the driver to be a friend of his father's, but did not understand what was going on. 'Uncle Sang, what's happening, where are we going?' he whimpered.

They turned off the highway. The skyscrapers had given way to dense jungle and the road followed the curve of a valley, culminating in a dead end. A dozen houses separated by rice paddies made up Mui Tse Lam village, five kilometres outside Sha Tin and fifty years behind the rest of Hong Kong. Chau's voice was laced with panic as he told his partner to take the boy to the house while he parked. He had not planned on Tak-sum seeing and recognizing him. The one-storey house was little more than a shack standing by itself at the base of a hill. When he reached the hut he realized their plan was crumbling—the door was locked. Seeing Chau and the boy standing outside on the veranda, Chan felt a wave of nausea. They had spent days scouting around for a hideout and the abandoned house had seemed ideal. His panic turned to rage and he lashed out at the boy, slapping him repeatedly across the face. Tak-sum screamed, cowering under his hands, and the commotion set off the village dogs. Within a minute the house was surrounded by a pack of mongrels. Afraid that the noise would alert the villagers, Chau scanned the path and neighbouring houses warily. One hundred yards behind the house was a dense wood. He grabbed Tak-sum by the arm and, telling Chan it would be safer in the trees, he dragged the boy up the path.

Chau called Tak-sum's father early that evening. He had been rehearsing his speech all afternoon. Trying to hide his nervousness, he boomed down the line: 'Are you waiting for your son to come home?' The father said he expected his son home any minute for dinner, but his stomach churned and he knew something was very wrong.

'We've got your son. Now listen carefully and don't ask any questions,' Chau said. The voice was familiar, but Lai couldn't place it and he listened in horror as the man demanded US$200,000 for his son's safe return. 'You've made a big mistake, I'm only a driver,' Lai said, stumbling over his words. 'I haven't got any money and I can't get that kind of cash from my family.'

'Just make sure you don't tell the police,' Chau warned. The voice was familiar, but still frustratingly out of memory's reach. 'We had thought of kidnapping you, but there's always someone with you, so we took your son. Cooperate with us and there'll be no trouble. I'll call again in twelve hours,' he said and hung up.

Lai's wife was at his side as he replaced the receiver and her eyes filled with tears as he told her what the man had said. Tak-sum was everything to her; she could not imagine life without him. The couple had no savings and with a combined monthly income of HK$2,700 there was no way they could meet the ransom demand. As she rocked back and forth, sobbing, Lai got back on the phone and arranged a family gathering.

Half an hour later his brother-in-law and aunt sat in the living room. The dinner grew cold on the stove as Lai told them what had happened and explained who he thought the caller was. His wife had heard him mention Chau Suk-sang, but she had never met him. Now Lai told them how he had worked with Chau four years earlier when he was with the Olympia Typewriter Company. They had been drivers together, but after a year Lai left to become a private chauffeur and he saw little of Chau—until recently. He had run into him four times in the last month. Lai was beginning to wonder whether those were chance meetings.

His aunt and brother-in-law comforted Lai's wife while he went to Chau's housing estate. He had no intention of confronting the man, but wanted to see if Chau was at home. He took a taxi to Ping Shek Estate and was dropped off outside a nearby McDonald's. Lai wandered through the multi-storey car park. He recognized the green saloon immediately and, without knowing what he was looking for, peered through the windows. The newspaper on the passenger seat gave away nothing and, uncertain what to do, he made a note of the licence number—BZ 2616.

On the way home he thought about how he had run into Chau the previous day. At the time he had assumed that bumping into him as he left work was coincidence and that the offer of a lift home was lucky. They had stopped at a cafe and over cups of jasmine tea Chau had told him about his new driving job and generous employer. On top of his basic salary, his boss gave him HK$1,500 a month to cover parking tickets. If he wasn't fined, he was allowed to pocket the money. Lai was impressed and asked how he had managed to land such a good job. At the time Lai hadn't thought much of Chau's answer, but now he saw the story in a different light. A kidnapping had united Chau with his new employer. The son of his wealthy boss had been abducted and Chau's cousin was one of the officers who helped rescue the boy. After the child was safely returned, the policeman advised the father to hire a driver who could double as a bodyguard, and he recommended Chau. By the time Lai returned home it was close to midnight. He and his wife decided to tell the police and Lai made the report in person. It was classified urgent and by 3am Chief Inspector Steve Vickers had been put in charge. Vickers, a sharp detective and a go-getter, was not used to dealing with kidnap victims who were so obviously poor. Usually they lived in mansions and were looked after by a household of servants, so he was surprised to see the impoverished father. Lai told him about the ransom demand and was insistent that the caller was his former colleague. Vickers took down Chau's address and sent Lai home with a Chinese inspector for support if the abductor called.

A full kidnapping team was assembled at police headquarters. Vickers and three of his men drove to Ping Shek Estate. It was 4am when they hammered on Chau's door and he answered, bleary-eyed and dishevelled. The police pushed past him and checked all the rooms, waking Chau's mother and his two children. His three-year-old daughter clung to his leg and when his one-year-old son began crying, it was Chau's mother who comforted the baby. His wife had deserted the family soon after their son's birth. A brief search of the flat and car turned up nothing incriminating and Chau was brought to the station for questioning.

It took two hours of interrogation before Chau would admit anything. The thirty-year-old said he had made the ransom demand, but insisted he knew nothing about the kidnapping. Vickers continued firing questions at him and after another hour he relented and gave Chan's name. Chan, he said, was the man behind the abduction. Chau agreed to help the police trap Chan and they returned to Ping Shek Estate with him. The detective stood over Chau as he paged Chan and left a message to meet him at noon at the Ho Moon Restaurant in Mong Kok.

Immediately north of Tsim Sha Tsui, the district of Mong Kok never sleeps. You can buy everything from CDs to sex on its streets, but beneath the neon veneer the city is decaying. The restaurant on Nelson Street, where Chau had arranged to meet his friend, was as dilapidated as its surroundings. The detectives drove Chau there in an unmarked police car just before 11am. He sat by himself at the back and the detectives chose a neighbouring table. The minutes passed slowly. Just after midday, Chan arrived. He hovered in the doorway as he surveyed the restaurant and, spotting his friend, walked over to him. As soon as he greeted Chau, the police pounced. Chan bolted into the toilet and the officers followed. The restaurant fell silent, chopsticks frozen in mid-air, as everyone listened to the scuffle in the men's room. Minutes later Chan was hustled out, his hands cuffed behind his back.

Chau and Chan were held in separate cells. In the early evening, Chau broke first, saying he wanted to tell the whole story. He admitted he had been in the car when the boy was kidnapped and had driven him to a village in the New Territories. He had dropped off Chan and Tak-sum and parked the car, returning just in time to see Chan and the boy disappearing into the woods. Chau was sure he had seen Chan grab the boy and throw him roughly onto the path. Chau said he ran back to the car and drove home. It was only later that day that Chan told him he had killed the boy and that he should make the ransom call.

First thing in the morning, Chau agreed to show the police where he had seen Chan hit the young victim. Chan followed in an unmarked police car. He had no idea what his friend had told the detectives. He kept quiet all the way to Mui Tse Lam, but when he saw Chau pointing out the woods he spoke up. He accused Chau of masterminding the plot and said he had only agreed to do it because he was desperate for money. Chau had told him he had a wealthy friend and that if they kidnapped the man's son they could demand a huge ransom. He explained how they had abducted the boy and driven him to the village. He said he had waited by the car while Chau took the boy into the woods. Chau had returned alone and said the boy had been 'fixed up'.

The detectives left Chan flanked by police and Chau led them into the woods, followed by a team of forensic experts and tracker dogs. A thick canopy of leaves blocked out the sun as the officers fought their way through the trees and bamboo, stumbling over gnarled roots. Three hundred metres into the wood, Chau pointed out a mound between two withered trees. This was Tak-sum's grave.

On their hands and knees, the police brushed away the leaves and loose soil. The boy's left leg was uncovered first, the skin pale and taut. He had been buried less than two days. Within minutes his whole body was exposed. He was clad only in white underpants and a vest, with faint bruises across his arms and chest. But it was the bruising on his face and neck that was the most severe. Dark purple marks stretched down the side of his face and his eyes were ringed with black. A mark running the length of his left side suggested he had been dragged along the ground. Fine bleeding marks spread like a rash across his face, a sure sign that he had been strangled.

Several Chinese newspaper reporters had followed the police, and photographers pushed aside the trees to get a better view of the body. Leaving the press and forensics team clustered around the body, Vickers frog-marched Chau back down the hill. Sitting in a police car, Chau gave yet another statement. This time he insisted his role had merely been as a lookout. He had gone part way into the woods and from a distance of about 15 metres he had seen Chan grab the boy's neck and throttle him. A few minutes later Chau loosened the boy's tie, took off his blazer, and buried him.

Later that evening Chau admitted he had thrown away the boy's clothes and school bag and agreed to show the police where he had dumped them. He also led the detectives to a nook in an embankment wall where he had stashed the school badge he had ripped off the boy's blazer, but he continued to deny that he had anything to do with the murder. He put all the blame on his partner and cast himself as the reluctant accomplice.

Chan also denied being the killer; he even had an alibi. His neighbours, a mother and her nineteen-year-old son, said they had been with him on the morning of 5 January. But a few days after they had made the claim, the police interviewed them under caution and they admitted they had lied. It would be left to the jury to decide where the guilt lay.

Meanwhile, Tak-sum's father was wrestling with questions of his own. Lai was haunted by the fear that it was he who had unwittingly made his son a target. In 1980, his rich uncle, Desmond Wong, had returned from the United States. Wong was Lai's idol: he had made it big in America, and was president of the World Trade and Shipping Organization. Wong was looking into investing in the Mainland's first Special Economic Zone, Shenzhen, and was considering spending US$300 million. Lai's mind boggled at the figure and he became excited when his uncle said there might be some work in it for him.

When Lai next ran into Chau, he couldn't help boasting about his uncle—it was rare that he had the opportunity to show off. Looking back, Lai realized his bragging may have cost him his son's life.

Chau's plan to help the police trap his partner failed. Instead of proving Chan guilty, he had incriminated himself. On 10 September 1982, he was sentenced to death. Chan was freed because there was not enough evidence to convict him.

Chau's appeal against his sentence was rejected, but he was not prepared to sit idly in prison. He spent the next fourteen years bombarding public figures with letters insisting he was innocent. He catalogued a series of allegations against the Legal Aid Department, the barrister who represented him, police officers, and even the judge. These letters were not all he penned from his prison cell. In 1994, he entered a Mother's Day poetry competition organized by a local radio station. The panel of judges were impressed with his entry. Applauded for his literary efforts, he took first prize and was named 'Best Son'. But Chau's fame was short-lived. Two days after congratulating the prisoner on his literary genius, the radio station discovered that his entry was the work of a famous Taiwanese poet. Chau was forced to return the prize.

New hope for Chau came in the form of Ludwig Ng, a devout Christian solicitor who had met Chau on one of his prison visits in 1990. The earnest lawyer listened to Chau's story and became convinced of his innocence. He offered his services for free and in 1993 began a lengthy bid to have the case reopened.

Ludwig Ng helped Chau petition the governor. He drew up an appeal which made a series of serious allegations. Chau claimed his trial had been unfair because the prosecution had withheld evidence and his defence had been poorly prepared. The petition was strong enough to persuade the governor and a re-investigation was ordered in July 1995. It was only the fourth time in Hong Kong's history that a Governor's Referral had been granted to reopen a case.

To ensure a thorough and independent investigation, a private security firm was hired. One of the firm's directors was Steve Vickers, who had left the police force a few years earlier. Having headed the investigation the first time around, Vickers knew the case inside out. He was unimpressed with Chau's allegations that the police had forced him to confess and that his statements had been dictated. Chau also claimed the police had promised his 'confessions' would only be used to trap Chan. He insisted he had not led the police to the body but that detectives had taken him to the scene.

The day before the retrial, Chau did an about-turn. He dropped his allegations and put forward a new appeal on technical grounds. He argued that by saying it was a case of 'murder or nothing', the judge had misdirected the jury. He demanded to be tried for manslaughter, not murder.

The appeal judge was furious. The trial had only been approved on the grounds of Chau's serious allegations. Even one of Chau's barristers, Gerard McCoy, branded him a 'detestable man who has defrauded us all'. With so much already invested in the appeal, it went ahead. Witnesses were recalled and the jury were taken to Mui Tse Lam to see where the boy had been killed. After three weeks in court, Chau was found guilty for the second time in thirteen years. He was sent back to prison to continue his life sentence.

The appeal had cost millions of dollars, but Governor Chris Patten defended his decision to grant a retrial. 'The Governor's power is there to be used to ensure that no miscarriage of justice can occur, but the decision is ultimately for the court,' Patten said. And the court had made its decision: Chau was guilty beyond a shadow of a doubt, guilty in 1982 and guilty again fourteen years later.

Sex Crimes

When the Chinese attack Western values, sexual permissiveness is often their chief complaint. Chinese tend to suppress the expression of sexuality for fear of creating disharmony. A more open attitude towards sex could create rifts within the family, say, if the parents disapproved of their child's choice of partner.

Oriental culture traditionally puts a high value on virginity in women. While many a young Hong Kong woman will have sex before she is married, it is usually with the man she believes will become her husband. This reticence is the reason that Hong Kong men are more likely to lose their virginity to a prostitute than a girlfriend.

Sex is not openly discussed in Hong Kong. Sex education is pushed to the bottom of the curriculum and largely concerns the mechanics of reproduction, with an emphasis on preventing unwanted teenage pregnancies. The limited time that the subject is permitted in schools does not allow for even the most cursory discussion of more complex issues.

In *Women in Society*, university lecturer Choi Po-king points out that the materials provided by the Education Department define sexual harassment as 'coercion to fulfil one's desires'. This explanation, Dr Choi says, 'misrepresents the common understanding among psychologists and counsellors that in most cases of sexual assault, the perpetrators are not motivated by desire, but by the wish to overpower through violence'.

Sexual gratification was not the motivation behind the sex murders that follow—both centred around power. Sex crimes are condemned in every culture, but they are especially abhorred in Hong Kong and have always been treated with contempt. When sex killer Au Yeung was taken to court in 1975, additional police security was needed to control the angry crowds of women who beat the side of his prison van. The trial had only just begun, but in the eyes of these women he was already guilty.

The Body in the Box: A Forensic First

Pan-pan was expecting her best friend to call, but when she did, she didn't sound herself. 'I'm at the tram station, bring me the tape straight away, a friend wants to borrow it,' she snapped and rang off. It wasn't like Yuk-ying to be so brusque, but Pan-pan supposed she must be late for class and hurried to the tram stop to meet her.

The Happy Valley tram terminus was their usual meeting place, only a five-minute walk from Pan-pan's home, and the stop Yuk-ying passed through on her way to her English lesson. Pan-pan clutched the tape, *Hits of Today*, in one hand and held her jacket together with the other; it was a cool December evening and although only 6.30pm, it was already dark. When she reached the terminus there was no sign of her friend. Across the road a café was serving tram drivers bowls of steaming noodles. She waited twenty minutes, stamping her feet against the cold, and, assuming her friend had gone to her lesson, went home.

The following morning, a street sweeper, finishing her rounds not far from where Pan-pan had stood, leaned her brush against the wall, put her hands on her hips, and surveyed the street. A large cardboard box, with the word 'Hitachi' printed in bold letters on the side, sat on the edge of the pavement. She had noticed the box in the doorway of a veterinary clinic a few hours earlier, but had thought nothing of it. Since it had been moved, she assumed it contained rubbish and pulled up a cardboard flap to take a peek.

'Wah, a dead dog!' she screamed, stumbling backwards. Her cry caught the attention of several passers-by, including a policeman. Without pausing for thought he, too, lifted the flap and peered inside. What he saw would stain his memory for years: the bloodied body of a naked young girl, curled in the foetal position, lay inside the box.

The body was identified the following day as Pin Yuk-ying, the youngest daughter of a large family and the darling of her household. Her parents were fishmongers who owned and ran a stall not far from their humble home near the harbour wall. The sixteen-year-old had left school and stayed at home to look after her two younger brothers, but she had been determined to get on in the world and hoped that learning English might be her ticket to a better life.

An autopsy revealed Yuk-ying had been strangled, a forearm locked around her neck from behind until she suffocated. The whites of her eyes and eyelids were stained with pinpoint bleeding marks—the telltale signs of asphyxiation—and deep, parallel scratch marks on either side of her neck bore testament to the short, but fierce, struggle she had put up. It was the injuries inflicted after her death that were the most horrific: both her nipples had been slashed, her right nipple more severely than the left, and her pubic region had been torched with a soldering iron. An examination revealed that her hymen was still intact; she was a virgin.

The case was given to Chief Inspector Derek Bere, known as Taffe to his friends. He was a charismatic detective, adored by the Chinese press for his offbeat ways and nicknamed 'Kojak' owing to his likeness to the popular TV detective. With his shaven, egg-shaped head and dark eyebrows, Bere neither looked nor acted like the average policeman. He had an outrageous sense of humour, a remarkable thirst, and was renowned for shouting 'yabadabadoo' whenever he entered a police mess. For all his quirks, he was a good detective, not least because he was unafraid of testing out his bizarre theories and laughing at himself when proven wrong.

The cardboard box was all the evidence Bere had to go on, but he soon discovered it held a wealth of information. There were also clues on the girl's body. Pieces of red paper and plastic with the Chinese characters for 'not soldered' had been found sticking to her elbow, so the detective told his team to look out for an electrical workshop. The pathologist discovered tiny fibres lodged under her fingernails and prepared slides to examine them more closely. He also found a strip of red plastic in her hair.

The box, with the model number printed on the side, originally housed a seventeen-inch black-and-white television. The Hitachi agents in Hong Kong gave police a list of the names and addresses of the 5,370 people who had bought the televisions, and 753 of them lived on Hong Kong Island. Armed with enlarged photographs of the

Derek Bere (right) receives a medal from former-HK Governor Sir Murray Maclehose

box, Bere's team were surprised at how many people had actually kept their boxes. They tracked down more than 100 owners, but the majority had either moved, without leaving a forwarding address, or discarded the boxes.

Bere decided it was time for one of his practical tests. He had an identical box made and persuaded a young policewoman, of similar weight to Yuk-ying, to lie in the box. She reluctantly took off her shoes and when she was curled up in the box, Bere tried to pick it up. He could only stumble a short distance with it and although it was fairly easy to carry with someone else's help, the box buckled under the weight. He then tried to see if it would fit in the boot of a number of cars, but it was too big to fit in most without the boot being left open. It was also too big for the interior of most cars, unless it was turned on its side, but this was ruled out as marks would have been left on the girl's body.

The detective concluded Yuk-ying had been killed close to where her body had been found. If the killer had gone to the effort of transporting the body, surely a remote area where it would have decomposed beyond recognition would have been a better dumping ground than a busy street. It was two weeks before Bere had his first break. He had told his team to interview everyone in the area and they were methodically working through a checklist of businesses and residents. While making enquiries at an ice cream shop opposite the tram station, one of his sergeants noticed a small workshop at the back. The shop's manager explained that the workshop was used to repair soft drink vending machines and invited him to have a look around.

A bare bulb lit the tiny room and the coils of wire and cable that cluttered the walls made it oppressive. The sergeant noticed a ball of coarse string on the workbench, similar to the bast fibre string used to secure the television box. Next to the string was a roll of white paper of the kind used for automatic teller machines, innocent enough, except that it was similar in width and texture to the paper stuck to Yuk-ying's elbow. The sergeant discreetly took samples of both and, as he was leaving, noticed a scrap of paper on the floor bearing the Chinese characters for 'repaired correctly'. He slipped this, too, in his pocket, along with a short length of copper wire and a scrap of plastic.

Bere completed the paperwork for a search warrant and asked one of his men to make discreet enquiries about the ice cream shop. It was owned by two brothers who employed fourteen people, all of whom worked days except for one man, Au Yeung, who ran the shop by himself from 6pm to 10pm. A couple of days later, Bere and his team raided the American Ice Cream Company. Au Yeung was alone in the shop, a pale, slightly built twenty-eight-year-old. He looked startled when Bere flashed his search warrant and demanded to know where the telephone was; Au Yeung pointed up a narrow staircase that led to a cock loft.

Bere negotiated the steep steps; the telephone was poised on a stack of directories and the detective had to bend awkwardly to see the dial, the numbers obscured by ballpen doodles. He nearly banged his head on a low beam as he extracted himself from the cock loft and, standing outside the workshop, asked Au Yeung to open the door. Au Yeung said he couldn't, it was a combination lock and he didn't know the number, but he offered to call the manager and within half an hour two mechanics arrived. They fixed the vending machines on a part-time basis and, throwing each other puzzled glances, unlocked the door and stood back to let Bere through. The workshop appeared harmless, it was certainly no torture chamber, but on a shelf below the workbench Bere found what he was looking for, an apparently harmless strip of red plastic, the same type of plastic found sticking to Yuk-ying's hair.

The workshop would need to be thoroughly searched, so Bere left a scientific evidence officer with his team and took Au Yeung off for questioning. Two officers would be stationed outside the ice cream shop that night to make sure no one tampered with the evidence. In a temporary field office near the tram terminus, Au Yeung explained that the ice cream shop was only an evening job; he worked as a clerk in a rattan shop during the day. He had taken on the second job after the birth of his daughter a year ago; the ice cream shop gave him an extra HK$300 a month which covered the cost of powdered milk and other necessities for the baby. His boss at the rattan shop had taken pity on him and let him leave work early so he could get to Happy Valley by 6pm. Working six days a week, from 9am until 10pm, he made just enough to support his wife and child.

With his translator in tow, Bere escorted Au Yeung home, a twenty-minute drive to Chai Wan on the east of Hong Kong Island. From the road, Au pointed out his flat, nestled in the middle of a series of drab concrete blocks. Au Yeung's wife answered the door. She held a baby under one arm and the crease of a frown marred her young face. Au Yeung ushered Bere inside, where a thin plywood partition separated the living room from two bedrooms. A man popped his head out from one of the bedroom doors and Au explained that he sublet a room to a young couple.

Bere asked Au Yeung's wife if she could remember what he had worn to work on 16 December. She pointed at the brown, checked jacket her husband was wearing, but said she couldn't remember which trousers he had worn. The detective was taking no chances, so he went into the bedroom and removed all of the suspect's clothes, twenty-nine pieces in total. His wife was close to frantic, but Au seemed unperturbed and even helped Taffe Bere put the clothes in a bag and returned to the Happy Valley field office for further questioning.

Au Yeung insisted he had never seen either the young girl who had been killed or the television box. Over the next twenty-four hours, Bere questioned Au Yeung about his life in intimate detail. He was a virgin until he met Kam-fung, the woman who would become his wife. He said he still loved her and insisted he never looked at other women, but admitted he was afraid of her. She could be lazy and bad-tempered and he usually gave in to her demands simply to keep the peace. His wife would sometimes visit him in the ice cream shop, as would his relatives, and on occasion they would use the telephone in the cock loft, but he never let customers use it. Bere had insufficient evidence to charge Au Yeung and after taking a long statement, he let him go.

While the Forensics Department was analysing the material from the workshop, Bere conducted another of his experiments. Again he recruited a young woman police constable and asked her to lie on the workshop floor. The cramped space meant that she had to rest her head and shoulders on the same wooden shelf on which the strip of plastic had been found. The detective then plugged the soldering iron into the socket under the workbench. Although the cable was long enough for the iron to reach the woman's groin, it could not reach her chest unless it was unplugged. This, Bere concluded, may have explained why the girl's pubic region had been torched, but not her breasts.

The forensics team had more conclusive evidence. They had scoured the workshop and even vacuumed the floor to collect loose debris. There was nothing unusual about what they collected—it was all fairly common material—but examined as a whole it left little doubt that the debris found in the box and stuck to Yuk-ying's body came from the workshop.

A chemist analysed the paint flakes found in the box and discovered that the paint was mixed; one sample showed grey paint over white and the other revealed two layers of white paint. The paint flecks corresponded with those found on the workshop floor and the double layer of paint narrowed the field, making the match more conclusive. Despite the mounting evidence, Taffe Bere found it hard to believe someone as timid as Au Yeung could be responsible for so horrendous a crime. There was no apparent motive, but the detective began to think otherwise after interviewing Au Yeung's wife. Although she was only twenty-one years old, she was headstrong and forceful in her opinions. She wasn't especially pretty, but she had youth on her side and was obviously used to getting her way. The young couple who sublet a room in the flat said they felt sorry for Au Yeung; his wife did nothing all day and when he returned home from work it was he who washed the baby's nappies and tidied the flat.

Bere asked Au Yeung's wife if she could remember how her husband had seemed on the night of the murder. She said he had seemed much himself, but was half an hour late, a delay he blamed on the traffic, and they went out to a late-night street café, or *dai pai dong*, for dinner. The following evening they were watching television when a report about the murder came on the news. Jokingly, she had said to her husband: 'The girl was killed so close to your shop, perhaps you did it.' Au Yeung had merely replied: 'I don't even know the girl and I haven't got a grudge against her; why should I kill her?' and then added: 'Even if I had wanted to kill her, how could I have done it by myself?'

Taffe Bere had to agree. Au had no obvious motive, but the evidence against him was persuasive. The most incriminating link was a blue and brown wool suit that Bere had taken from a hook on the back of Au Yeung's bedroom door. The blue fibres varied in shade from lilac to blue-black, and the Forensics Department produced a thorough report that showed that two lilac wool fibres found under Yuk-ying's fingernails were identical to the lilac fibres of the suit. In addition, three blue wool fibres, removed with sticky tape from the girl's back, and brown fibres, retrieved from her right leg, were identical to fibres from the suit. The colour of the blue fibres was intense enough to extract the dye, and chemical tests proved that the fibres from the suit and those found on the girl were indistinguishable. The lab's findings were further strengthened by finding two alien green fibres on the sleeve of the jacket that were identical to four green fibres found on the girl's body and in the box.

Almost four months after the murder, Bere felt he had enough evidence for a conviction and on 27 March 1975, he arrested Au Yeung. He banged on his door early in the morning and Au Yeung, clad only in track suit bottoms, answered. His thin, hairless chest and pale face still creased with sleep made him look a pathetic creature. The rest of the household lay in bed, listening, as he was arrested and charged with murder. Bere waited for him to wash and dress and five minutes later, when he was ready to leave, a pallid, emotionless calm had replaced his initial startled expression. Au Yeung retained that calm as he stood before the magistrate in Central. 'I did not kill anyone,' he said simply, but his request for bail was refused and he was taken to prison where he spent the weeks preceding the trial.

The trial lasted three weeks and a jury of five men and three women were taken painstakingly through the more than 250 exhibits. Forensic evidence was a relatively new concept in Hong Kong courts in the

1970s, and pathologists and chemists explained the basic procedures of sampling and analysis. The jury were shown slides of the fibres and paint flecks and allowed to make comparisons themselves.

The jury heard how Au Yeung's wife had jokingly suggested he had killed the girl since the murder occurred so near his workplace. Asked if the conversation had been accurately recalled, Au Yeung simply said: 'I told my wife that if I had carried out the murder, I was a very capable man.'

The newspapers covered the court case daily and a few days into the trial, a nineteen-year-old woman picked up a paper and stared in horror at the front-page photo of Au Yeung. She immediately recognized the man who had twice burnt her with a cigarette. The first time, just under two years earlier, she had been waiting for a bus when two girls nudged her and told her that the man standing behind her had burnt holes in her skirt. She twisted her skirt around, saw several perfect circles burnt into the hem of her skirt, and scolded the man. He ignored the girls, simply raising his newspaper to blot them from view, a cigarette butt smouldering by his foot. Six months later, she was waiting at the same bus stop when she felt a burning sensation on her thigh. She swung around and saw the same man behind her. He had a lit cigarette in his hand and she noticed she had several holes in the hem of her miniskirt. This time she was alone; she threw him a nasty look but said nothing. She said she had seen him since at the bus stop and always made a point of keeping her distance.

The woman was convinced it was Au Yeung who had burnt her and went to the police, but her evidence was unwittingly jeopardized by an overzealous junior inspector. Keen to show Bere that he could do more than take statements, the inspector recorded the woman's complaint and then went ahead with a photo identification on his own. He spread seven pictures on the desk and asked the woman to point out her assailant. Without hesitation she picked out the shot of Au Yeung, but in the inspector's haste he had chosen six black-and-white photos, while the one of Au Yeung was in colour. Au Yeung's lawyers complained that the photo identification was unfair and it was thrown out of court.

Au Yeung had kept his cool throughout the trial, repeatedly and calmly denying that he had anything to do with the murder, but on the penultimate day he became almost hysterical. He began by insisting he was the victim of an unfortunate coincidence, that, by chance, the killer was wearing the same clothes as he was, which explained the matching fibres. To prove that he was caught in an unlucky cycle, he began ranting that there were four 'thirteens' linked to his trial: the serial number on the television box was thirteen; the newspaper found in the box was dated 13 December 1974; the time recorded on his punch-card for 16 December was 10.13pm; and it was the thirteenth day of the trial that day. 'Four' is unlucky for the Chinese, as the Cantonese word for the number sounds similar to the word for 'death', and thirteen is considered unlucky in the West, so Au Yeung considered his fate extremely unfortunate and was desperate for the jury to recognize this. But after weeks of timid behaviour, his bizarre appeal only had a negative effect.

In summing up, the judge said to the jury that although there was no clear motive, they could surely imagine a reason for the killing and he told them to carefully consider the wealth of forensic evidence. On 3 November, after three-and-a-half hours of deliberation, the jury returned a verdict of guilty. It was the first time in Hong Kong that someone had been convicted purely on forensic evidence. Au Yeung was calm as the verdict was read out and he showed no flicker of emotion as the judge sentenced him to death.

His sentence was automatically commuted to life imprisonment and within three months Au Yeung had sought an appeal. His lawyer complained that by saying there was no reason for a motive but that one could be imagined, the judge had encouraged the jury to speculate and endangered a fair trial. He also criticized the investigation for focusing entirely on Au Yeung as soon as he fell under suspicion and slammed detectives for not analysing the clothing of other employees.

It was with reluctance that the judge quashed Au Yeung's conviction and set aside his sentence. Au spent the months prior to the retrial in jail, but his wife visited him regularly, bringing their young daughter with her. She was convinced of her husband's innocence and his plight had softened the rough edge with which she had always treated him. She sat in the public gallery during his retrial and was in tears when, for the second time in six months, he was sentenced to death. On this occasion the judge took the time to commend the homicide team and Bere in particular for the most thorough investigation he had ever come across.

Au Yeung's wife was still convinced her husband was no killer and called a press conference in a tea house. It was Au Yeung's brother who addressed the press, speaking in a confident voice, raised to be heard over the noise of the traffic outside. He counted off on his fingers the reasons for another retrial: there was no motive for the murder; Au Yeung's fingerprints were never found on the box; fibres found on the girl's body could not be relied on as evidence; and Au Yeung had not worn the incriminating suit for at least two weeks before the murder—even his neighbours were willing to confirm that.

Au Yeung made headlines again on 8 August 1976—'Au Yeung loses second appeal over murder'—only this time he was relegated to the inside pages, as the press tired of this long-running saga. As the press became less interested, so Au Yeung became more emotional. The timid clerk who had stared blankly into the faces of law makers, jurors, and the curious now shouted to onlookers as he was led to a prison van: 'I didn't kill the girl. I do not feel guilty at all although I have been convicted.'

Prison gave Au Yeung the chance for an education and he spent his time locked in a cell with his head buried in a book. He became fluent in English, devoured literary classics, and took an accountancy course, qualifying as an accountant after years of study. Throughout his imprisonment, he had always maintained his innocence but, thirteen years after his second failed appeal, he spoke out publicly from prison and admitted his guilt: he had killed Yuk-ying.

Bere has long since retired, but he has not forgotten the case. When told that Au Yeung had finally admitted his guilt, the former detective merely raises his eyebrows and sighs, a reserved gesture for one as gregarious as Bere. Although Au Yeung never explained why he had killed the girl, Bere has a theory about what happened that night. He suspects that the girl had asked to use the phone and that Au Yeung had shown her to the cock loft. Aroused at the sight of the teenager bending over to use the phone, he had impulsively tried to touch her and she had screamed. In an attempt to keep her quiet, Bere reckons Au Yeung had put his hand over her mouth, his arm around her neck, and the more she had struggled the more he had squeezed. He had killed her by accident. Terrified when he realized she was dead, Bere suspects he had undressed her to remove any contact evidence, and then tried to make it look like the work of a sex maniac by slashing her nipples and burning her. He may well have found the television box discarded nearby and dumped the girl on the doorstep of the veterinary clinic, hoping the cleaner would assume it was a dead dog and send it to the incinerator.

In a sunlit bar on the coast of Spain, a drinking hole that Bere refers to as his new headquarters, the former detective sips sangria and muses over the case. He still has the volumes of fibres, paint, and other forensic evidence that was produced in court, a legacy of one of his biggest cases. As he flicks through the files he wonders aloud whether the murder would have happened had Au Yeung's wife been a kinder woman. 'She was a right battle-axe, that woman,' laughs Bere as he leans across the counter and, in a conspiratorial half whisper, says: 'He was the only murderer I really felt sorry for.'

Braemar Hill—Double Murder

Three hundred and fifty officers stood on the brow of the hill, heads bowed and faces creased in concentration. Slowly they inched forward, methodically scouring the undergrowth. The sheer number of men showed that something about this case was different. Nothing would be left to chance and the massive search party began at first light. As they painstakingly made their way down the valley, they took the first steps in what would become a long trail to find those responsible for one of Hong Kong's most horrendous murders.

It was not the brutality of this double slaying that made it such a high-profile case. It was the racial implications. The victims were Westerners. That's not to say the case would not have been thoroughly investigated had the victims been Chinese, but it would never have commanded the degree of manpower and attention that two British youths did. This was 1985, the handover to China was well over a decade away and Hong Kong lived up to its colonial reputation. The British may not have been revered by the Chinese, but they were still afforded a grudging respect. For the most part, local Chinese and Westerners succeeded in living side by side with as limited interaction as possible. There was no open hostility, but a tacit acknowledgment of the 'them' and 'us' divide. This senseless murder was out of kilter with the rhythm of the city and the expatriate population was thrown into panic.

The endearing idealism of the victims made their deaths all the more poignant. In a city where teenagers are notoriously politically apathetic, Kenneth McBride and Nicola Myers saw beyond the narrow confines of a fast-decaying colonialism. They wanted an end to apartheid, a healthy environment, and world peace. It was these shared dreams that brought them together.

Everyone at Island School knew Kenneth. As president of the students' union he had been the voice of his peers, and he had shown his strength and stamina captaining the rowing team. But for all his gregarious energy, he had a more sensitive side. He would write poetry in his spare time, sometimes with his girlfriend Nicola. They made a good couple, not least of all because of their good looks. Nicola was especially attractive. She was eighteen, a few months older than Kenneth, and had big brown eyes and wavy shoulder-length hair. Both were facing their A level exams and would study together. He had been offered a place at Edinburgh to study politics and history. Nicola focused on languages, hoping to become an interpreter, perhaps for the United Nations.

When they set off for a walk on a Saturday afternoon in April, they had their whole lives ahead of them. Their only concern was for their upcoming exams. They took their textbooks with them, Kenneth cradling his in his left arm because a sports injury had put his right arm in a sling. The couple left after lunch, telling their parents they were going to find a quiet spot to study. That was the last time they were seen alive.

When they did not return home that evening, their parents were worried and went out looking for them. They searched the hillside, calling out their names over the din of the cicadas, but there was no answer. First thing in the morning, they returned to the hill and this time found the text books. They immediately called the police, but they were not the first to raise the alarm. A hiker had made the gruesome discovery of the bodies during his early morning walk.

Chief Inspector Norrie MacKillop was handed the case. MacKillop joined the Hong Kong Police in 1976, when the force was undergoing upheavals to stamp out corruption. He was a new breed of officer, thorough in his investigations and careful about the rules. Police in those days were not averse to using force during interrogations, but slowly MacKillop showed the benefits of a gentler approach. Psychopaths and brutal murderers, he said, often did not realize what they had done was wrong. Putting an arm around them and offering a cup of tea could extract a confession more easily than resorting to violence, he insisted.

Detective Inspector Peter Ip Pau-fuk knew there was trouble before MacKillop called. From his flat he could see ambulances and police cars tearing up the road, sirens blaring. MacKillop arranged to meet him at Braemar Hill. It was already swarming with police and reporters when they arrived. Breaking free of the press pack, they made their way up the hill. The bodies lay a short distance apart on a steep slope, just over 40 yards from where the parents had found the school books. Kenneth's hands were tied behind his back. His body was covered in cuts and had dark bruises across his neck. Nicola's injuries were more severe; it was obvious she had been beaten for some time. Her body was covered with 500 abrasions and lacerations. She was naked. Ip ran back to his car to get a piece of canvas to cover her body.

MacKillop sat in on the post-mortem. He always found it the grimmest part of a case but felt it important to be there to ask questions. This one was his most harrowing. Analysing the contents of Kenneth's stomach, the pathologist estimated that he had died in the late afternoon. He had put up a struggle, but with only one able arm he had been quickly overpowered and tied up. A wooden pole had been forced down on his neck until he suffocated. Nicola died a couple of hours after her boyfriend. Her end had been more horrific. She had been raped, beaten, and tortured. It was a final blow to her head that had killed her.

The next day the search began in earnest. The police suspected that the killers were young thugs; professionals would have known that attacks on Westerners only spell trouble. No expense was spared and 350 officers combed the hillside looking for evidence. The slope was scrutinized so closely that even a buckle from Nicola's bra and her bracelet were discovered. Her clothing was found scattered around the area. Not far from the murder site was a rock pool. A few pages torn from a French textbook lay scattered on the ground. The detectives saw something at the bottom of the murky pool, so Ip stripped off, plunged into the water, and surfaced holding a wooden rod. One end was splintered and the other was covered with blood. The blood had congealed with the mud to give a dark green colour. On the opposite bank they found the other half of the rod. A few hairs were caught in the splintered end, and analysis showed them to be Nicola's.

The rod was their first real clue. If fingerprints could be lifted from the murder weapon, they would be well on their way to catching the killers. Fingerprint identification is based on a points system, with a minimum number of points needed to confirm a match. But Hong Kong did not have the technology for such tests, so the rod was sent to London. The official police line is that the London lab could not detect enough points to make an identification. But a British officer based in the control room and responsible for the case's administrative work told a different story. He said that a number of the officers, unfamiliar with the fingerprinting process, had unwittingly touched the rod and jeopardized it as a piece of useful or conclusive evidence.

Despite the massive search, the police were no closer to the finding the killers. They set up a hotline and appealed for information, no matter how trivial; they suspected a number of robberies and assaults in the area had gone unreported, and if the victims spoke up, they might be able to provide valuable leads. Then they heard of a rape two weeks before the murders. A British woman, the wife of a senior police officer, had been assaulted. She had been walking her dog on Braemar Hill, as she did every day, when she was overpowered by a Chinese man. The rape was brutal and, police suspected, premeditated. Distraught after the attack, she had chosen not to report it. Police suspected this man might be the link to the murders.

All the local papers reported the murders on Monday. Soon few in Hong Kong had not heard of the brutal killings, but after several days the Chinese press took a different tack from the English-language papers. Rather than simply keeping abreast of the investigation and giving details of the victims' lives, they raised a number of sensitive issues. The Sino-British Joint Declaration on the Future of Hong Kong, an agreement finalizing the territory's return to the Mainland, had been signed six months earlier. Negotiations between the two sides had been fraught, and the Chinese press questioned whether the killings might have a political motive. The investigation itself came under heavy criticism. The police were accused of devoting unnecessary manpower and public funds merely because the victims were white. There were calls of racism.

It fell to Brian Merritt, head of the Organized and Serious Crime Bureau, to calm jitters and defend the investigation. Merritt was a tall man with a heavy-set jaw and an almost military assertiveness. His confident manner had won him few friends on the force, but his authoritative style was just right for the job. During a heated press conference, a Chinese reporter demanded to know why so much was being spent on the case and accused Merritt of racism. Merritt rose to the occasion. He insisted race was not the issue, citing his concern in cases where the victims had been locals. He defended the use of funds, saying the brutality of the murders warranted such a response. Merritt, meanwhile, continued to keep the murders in the public eye. During the five months after the murders, he released details of the investigation a little at a time in an attempt to keep it front-page news. It was the most controversial murder of his career and he was determined that he would be seen to have it solved.

Days after the murder, police offered a reward. Fifty thousand dollars was a reasonable sum, but months went by and there were no takers. Perhaps a bigger reward would get someone to talk, Merritt mused. Soliciting for a reward was strictly against the books, but if it brought the killers to justice surely it was justified. Besides, the pressure was mounting and he needed to conclude the case. One of Merritt's men was a mysterious character, but he had interesting contacts, and with Merritt's blessing, this officer had a chat with a wealthy businessman. He showed him police photos of the teenagers taken at the scene and suggested he offer a higher reward 'for the good of the Hong Kong people'. The pictures were enough to persuade the businessman. Requesting anonymity, he bumped up the reward to HK$500,000. It was the biggest reward that had ever been offered in a murder case in Hong Kong.

Five months into the investigation the police were no nearer to catching the killers. Neither the mobile command unit at Braemar Hill, nor the door-to-door interviews, nor a new computer system had yielded any leads. Then they came across a group of youths who seemed to fit the bill. The gang was made up of young thugs who would beat and rape their victims. MacKillop was determined to play it cool, bring in the kids, and take it from there. When Merritt heard the team were onto something he was ecstatic; more than anyone he felt the pressure to get a conviction. There were to be no mistakes. A series of raids were carefully planned and the gang was arrested. MacKillop interviewed the youths individually. He began as though he had all the time in the world, and then he got specific. The gang members were suspects in eight unrelated rape and assault incidents and MacKillop wanted to know if they were involved. One by one they admitted their guilt. And then he threw in the big one: Braemar Hill. The response was unanimous. No. Absolutely not. They were not that kind of gang. MacKillop believed them. He had carefully honed his interview technique and was convinced they were telling the truth. They were rapists, and violent ones at that, but they were not the killers.

This was not what Merritt wanted to hear. He had convinced himself the gang was responsible—after all, it was unusual to have two gangs doing the same thing. Eager for a result, Merritt had already told the Commissioner of Police that they had found the killers. MacKillop was angry. It seemed the pen-pushers were trying to call the shots. If the gang was held responsible for the murders, not only would it be an injustice, but the real culprits would get away. A clash was inevitable and when Merritt told him to 'just get a confession out of them', he was furious. Beating confessions out of suspects was not MacKillop's style. He stood firm. 'With respect,' he told Merritt, 'these aren't your guys.'

It was a further agonizing three months before MacKillop was proved right. An informer—one of the obsequious characters that police refer to as their 'walking ears'—landed the big break. He happened to overhear a rowdy group of young men at a ferry pier. The conversation was dominated by Pang Shun-yee, a twenty-four-year-old with a cocky swagger. Pang was boasting that he had killed a Western couple. Some of the others mocked him, doubting his tale. They demanded that he prove it. 'Look at my trainers,' he said, 'They belonged to the dead boy.' The informant could not believe his luck. Keeping a safe distance, he followed Pang back to his home and then rushed off to tell the team.

After days of surveillance, Pang and his gang were arrested by more than 100 Organized Crime and Triad Bureau officers. MacKillop knew he had the right gang this time; the next step was to make sure they were convicted. Sure enough, Pang's trainers had belonged to Kenneth. They were a size nine, Kenneth's size, and on top of the impression that Kenneth's foot had made in each shoe was Pang's smaller one. The shoes may have been incriminating, but they were not enough to prove Pang guilty. MacKillop knew he would have to get one of the others to talk. At fifteen, Won Sam-lung was the youngest of the five and MacKillop suspected he would be the easiest to work on. There was no need for violence or threats—MacKillop, with great patience, simply sat and listened. Piece by piece he coaxed the story out of the teen.

Won said one of his friends lived in Shau Kei Wan and they had been walking to his house over Braemar Hill when they saw the couple. The pair were talking and had not noticed them, so they decided to 'have some fun' with them and see if they had any money. They split into two groups and approached from different directions. The couple were startled and when they said they didn't have any money, the gang tied them up. Then one of them 'sprang onto the woman like a hungry dog'. It was Pang, Won said, who suggested they kill the couple, fearing they might be able to identify them later. They killed Kenneth first and then they turned on Nicola. They beat and tortured her for 'dozens of minutes'. She was still breathing faintly when they left.

Raped, abused, and tortured, Nicola had died alone. MacKillop managed to keep his cool, for without Won's confession he knew their evidence was poor. In September 1986, Won's statement incriminating his friends was read to the court. Four months later the second youngest in the gang, Cheung Yau-hang, who was sixteen at the time of the murders, confessed. He said he had taken part in the attacks, but only because Pang had told him to. With Won's evidence, there was little doubt in the jury's mind. Pang and the two elders in the group, Tam Sze-foon and Chiu Wai-man, were sentenced to death. Their appeal was rejected but two years later their sentences were commuted to life.

The investigation took its toll on MacKillop. With a daughter of his own, he was confronted with the fears that every parent has for his or her child. After the case was solved he completed a master's degree, and when he returned to the force he switched to the narcotics department. He had had enough of homicide.

Over the Border

Hong Kong's closest neighbours, Guangzhou to the north and Macau to the east, both have a wild streak running through them. Across the border from Hong Kong, Shenzhen, China's first Special Economic Zone, has become a huge success, but the city shows the signs of growing up too fast: corruption and prostitution. With all these cities just a short distance away, Hong Kong cannot help but be affected.

The early 1990s saw the rise of mainland gangsters whose furtive forays into Hong Kong were invariably marked by violence. There was no shortage of firepower in those days. The People's Liberation Army had demobbed 1.3 million soldiers and was changing weapons, from AK-47s to AK-49s and .54 pistols to .59s. The combined effect of cutbacks and upgrades meant a surplus of cheap guns on the black market: an AK-47 could be bought for HK$3,000 and a Russian-made hand grenade cost just HK$300. With easy access to such weapons, it is not surprising that the criminals who slipped across the border were armed to the teeth.

The two most notorious were Yip Kai-foon and Cheung Tze-keung, the latter better known as Big Spender. Many of the men in Yip Kai-foon's gang were ex-Chinese army soldiers and their military training had equipped them well for armed robbery.

The Cultural Revolution also played a role in shaping these men. During those anarchic years between 1966 and 1976, schools were closed, teachers attacked, and diligent students accused of lacking 'revolutionary spirit'. Power fell into the hands of teenagers claiming allegiance to Chairman Mao. Known as the Red Guards, these youngsters wielded power beyond their years and it is not surprising that they abused this power to terrorize anyone they disliked or envied. Traditional family values collapsed as children were encouraged to denounce their own mothers and fathers as counter-revolutionaries. Many youngsters were left to fend for themselves while their parents were detained for political re-education.

As urban youths sent to the countryside returned to the cities, many found themselves without hope of education or employment. Crime was a lucrative option for some members of this lost generation and, if nothing else, the Cultural Revolution had qualified them for the job. The chaos of the uprising and disregard for authority had shaken the foundations of their world. They had been left with no respect for parents or teachers, and feared nothing.

Superintendent Gregory Lam Kwai-bun has dedicated enough years of his life to front-line duty to make him an authority on mainland gangsters. Now safely tucked behind a desk in police headquarters, the portly superintendent says many of the gangsters who made their way to Hong Kong in the early 1990s had violent backgrounds. A good number had been Red Guards. Lam says poverty and politics have conspired to make murder less of a crime on the Mainland. 'Life is cheaper in China because they have seen so many people die. For them, killing someone is not as great a crime as it is in the West.'

While mainland gangsters plagued Hong Kong in the early 1990s, Macau caused no trouble. Life there was tranquil, despite the fact that 15,000 of Macau's population of 500,000 are estimated to be triads. For decades the gangsters had run their vice operations peacefully alongside the Portuguese administration. The triads got a foothold in the casinos when Stanley Ho—founder of the Sociedade de Turismo e Diversoes de Macau (STDM) and controller of the enclave's gaming monopoly—began franchising out private VIP rooms and taking commissions on the earnings. These rooms are where big money changes hands and 'high rollers' often play for six-figure stakes. The triads jumped at the chance to run the VIP rooms; on top of the gambling, they could get money from loan sharking and prostitution. Stanley Ho had offered the triads a legitimate interest in the casinos. This coexistence has worked to the benefit of all concerned. Macau's biggest industry is gambling, accounting for half its gross domestic product, and triads operate from all ten of the enclave's casinos.

The 14K are Macau's most influential triad syndicate, and the Wo On Lok run a close second. Between the two, they have stakes in most of the enclave's gambling. The Sun Yee On have only a small say in the casinos and the 14K and Wo On Lok have long contrived to keep it that way. The delicate balance was destroyed in late 1996 when the 14K and the Wo On Lok, hoping to be in the best position to take over the gambling franchise after the 1999 handover of Macau to China, began scrambling for power. The gang rivalry coincided with the property market crash: 50,000 houses and offices were left vacant that year. Feeling the economic pinch, the triads relied heavily on the casinos for income and the result was an explosive period of several years in which triad turf wars rocked the usually peaceful enclave.

13

Yip Kai-foon and Big Spender: The Wild East

When people think of Yip Kai-foon, they think of an image caught by a security camera: he stands braced outside a gold shop wearing a balaclava, with an AK-47 slung over his shoulder. That picture, shown again and again, is a reminder of the time in the early 1990s when open gun battles with police took place on crowded Hong Kong streets. It was the start of a bloodthirsty frenzy that saw Yip Kai-foon link up with another notorious gangster on a set of kidnappings that culminated in the killing in broad daylight of a fellow gangster turned informant.

Yip Kai-foon was from Chao Zhou (Chiu Chow), a region in north-east Guangdong Province. The people there, renowned for fierce loyalty and fiery tempers, are notoriously shrewd in business and can be tight with their money, but they always look after their own kind. Yip Kai-foon was Chao Zhou to the core, a fearless gangster for whom pillaging and plundering were second nature. He was born in Haifeng, not far from the coast, and grew up to fulfil the Chao Zhou saying: 'In the sky there is the God of Thunder, on earth there are Haifeng and Lufeng'. For half a dozen years, Yip Kai-foon was Hong Kong's own God of Thunder.

Yip first came to the attention of police in 1984, when they were trying to track down the booty from a watch shop robbery. An informant told the police about a gang selling valuable watches on the black market, and they spent weeks setting up a meeting. Two officers posed as buyers and Yip Kai-foon agreed to meet them near the Wan Chai waterfront. It was early evening and they had only the car headlights to see by. As soon as Yip produced the goods, the officers arrested him. They took the gun that was tucked into his belt and hustled him into a police car. But Yip was not one to go down without a fight and he whipped out a pistol that he had strapped to his ankle. He would have shot both policemen and fled, but one of the officers jammed his finger behind the trigger and wrestled the pistol away from him.

The police were convinced that Yip and his gang were responsible for the robbery, but they didn't have enough evidence to prove it. Nevertheless, they had plenty to charge Yip with. He was eventually sentenced to eighteen years for handling stolen property, firearms offences, and resisting arrest. The police were satisfied that they would not be seeing Yip Kai-foon for a long time. How wrong they were.

Prisons worldwide have a history of doing more than merely detaining offenders—they serve as schools for criminals and a meeting place for those in the business. While Yip Kai-foon was doing time in Stanley Prison, he got to know fellow mainland gangster Cheung Tze-keung. Better known as Big Spender, Cheung would later carry out the world's biggest cash robbery and mastermind the kidnapping of the children of two of Hong Kong's wealthiest tycoons. Yip was the yang and Cheung was the yin (active and passive forces) and together they made the perfect criminal partnership.

Cheung had been jailed for forging identity cards, a fairly innocuous start to his criminal career. Yip was six years Cheung's junior but the more gung-ho of the two. Yip would become known for being trigger-happy, Cheung for being a planner—his crimes were always well thought out. Given that Cheung's risks were so carefully calculated, it came as no surprise that he was an avid gambler. He liked nothing better than to spend an evening in a casino and later, when he had money to burn, he would play the high roller and fly around the world gambling.

After Cheung's release from prison, Yip was desperate to get out. He was a man of action and unprepared to spend the rest of his life cooped up in jail; he was willing to risk everything to be free. On 22 August 1989, he sat doubled over in his cell complaining of chronic stomach pains and was rushed to Queen Mary Hospital with suspected appendicitis. The hospital is in a relatively isolated spot on the western tip of Hong Kong Island, with a mountain behind and the sea in front. The custodial ward was full, so Yip was taken to a ward just off the main prisoners' section.

Cheung Tze-keung rejoices after winning a court appeal

Considered dangerous, Yip was handcuffed and accompanied by two armed guards, but he was allowed visitors, and his brother came to see him. They chatted for half an hour and when his brother had left, Yip said he needed to go to the toilet. He was escorted to the urinals and on the way he asked if he could take his handcuffs off to use the toilet. One of the guards grudgingly agreed and released Yip. When he went to refasten the handcuffs, Yip grabbed a glass bottle from a cabinet and smashed it on the edge. Gripping the neck of the bottle he lunged at the guards, threatening them with the broken glass. They stumbled backwards and Yip bolted out the door.

Yip sprinted down the corridor and the guards gave chase. They blew their whistles, but their guns remained firmly in their holsters—this was no place to let off a round of bullets. Reaching the ground floor, Yip ran across the foyer. Through the large glass doors he could see the driveway leading to the main road. The queue at the taxi rank scattered as Yip swung open the doors and ran up to a car that had pulled up at the concourse. A middle-aged man was in the driver's seat and a young boy in the back. Yip jumped in the back, grabbed the boy, and threatened him with the broken bottle. He ordered the man to drive.

The driver kept an eye on his son in the rear-view mirror as he followed Yip's instructions. When they reached the main road, Yip ordered him to turn left, towards Aberdeen. Five minutes down the road, Yip told him to pull over, take off his shorts and T-shirt, and toss them back to him. Yip snatched the clothes and ordered the man to continue driving. They passed a housing estate on their left, then a cemetery; on their right was the sea. The road ran through an industrial area crammed with factories and warehouses, the pavements were crowded, and the traffic shuffled between sets of lights. Yip ordered the man to stop the car, demanded money from him, and fled. The man watched as Yip raced down the street and jumped on a bus.

Yip's dramatic escape immortalized him. It was Asia's Wild West story and the media savoured it. He was a gangster without fear and, as Hong Kong was soon to discover, he did not intend to hang up his gun. After a brief sojourn in Guangdong, Yip began planning his next venture. It took him several months to renew his contacts in the underworld and secure weapons. Less than a year after his escape, Yip was back in business.

Kwun Tong is the real Hong Kong, the working man's heart of the city. It is an attractive but functional district. Above the chaos of commerce and commuters on the street, the high-rise buildings are home to thousands. In the centre of Kwun Tong, Mut Wah Street hums with life. The shops spill out onto the street, herbalists display tubs of dried seafood, and fruit sellers stand behind pyramids of oranges. At the end of the street, on the right, is an old market, and beneath the corrugated roofs sprawls a labyrinth of poky shops. Brown padded bras are stacked six feet high and there are piles of pyjamas and flip-flops. Opposite is a cluster of gold shops and jewellers, thriving on the healthy competition. Their proximity makes it easy for consumers to compare prices. For gangsters, it is easier to raid several jewellers in one hit.

On 9 June 1991, Yip and his gang of six stole a car and headed to Kwun Tong. They pulled up outside the string of jewellery shops on the main drag. It was late afternoon and the street was crowded with school children, housewives, and labourers. Dressed in black, a balaclava pulled over his head, Yip Kai-foon jumped out of the car and stood with his back to the jewellers. Training an AK-47 up and down the street, he took control of the pavement. The rest of the gang ran into the jewellers' shops, firing warning shots above their heads. Sales assistants dropped to the floor and cowered behind the glass-topped counters. Ignoring the cases of silver, the gang went only for gold, snatching necklaces, bracelets, and rings. Within minutes the police arrived and Yip and his gang fired at the officers. The police returned the gang's fire and people scattered as the street became a war zone. This was no foolhardy gang. They were professionals and they moved as though they had military training—one gangster would fire to cover another as he ran. Their bags weighed down with jewellery, they fled behind a screen of bullets, escaping with more than HK$5.7 million in gold.

Flush with success, Yip began making plans for similar robberies, but it was Cheung who made the next move. Unlike Yip, who favoured brute force, Cheung Tze-keung preferred a more calculated approach. His robbery would be on a much larger scale than Yip's and had been months in the making.

Early one morning in July 1991, three gunmen held up a Guardforce security van outside Kai Tak Airport. The guards were tied up, thrown in the back of the van, and driven to Kowloon Bay, a few minutes away. There, ten bags of cash, in US and Hong Kong dollars, were transferred to another van. The gang escaped with HK$167 million, the largest cash robbery in history, and made headlines around the world. Cheung and his gang did not get far, however; within days police had tracked them down to their hideout in the New Territories.

The timing of the robbery had been perfect and police suspected that inside information must have been leaked for the gang to have known the exact moment such an unusually large sum of money was being transferred. Cheung's girlfriend was an immediate suspect. Not only had she worked for Guardforce for eighteen months, she was also in the Kai Tak control room at the time of the robbery. She was charged with aiding and abetting a robbery, but the charge had to be dropped because of insufficient evidence.

Cheung was convicted for the robbery, given an eighteen-year sentence, and returned to Stanley Prison. While he waited to appeal his conviction, he got to know more of Hong Kong's infamous criminals, including the loan shark Wong Kwai-fun. In 1995, the Court of Appeal overruled his conviction on the grounds that his identification by key witnesses was unreliable and their overall evidence was contradictory. The following year he was retried and acquitted. Cheung was a free man and there was no hiding his happiness. He walked out of the High Court with his hands raised and spoke to reporters with confidence. It was the beginning of his affair with the press. Later he would hold impromptu conferences with reporters to complain about police harassment and brutality, posing for photographers in front of his Lamborghini.

Meanwhile, Yip and his gang had been busy doing what they did best: armed robberies. Eight months after hitting the jewellery shops in Kwun Tong, they did the same thing in Hung Hom, also on Kowloon side. Again they barged into gold shops armed to the teeth, helped themselves to the jewellery, and fled under a hail of bullets. Yip's sheer nerve helped carry them through the raid, and the gang's speed and organization ensured success. Police scrutinized footage of the robbery taken by the shops' security cameras and were confident that the gang had army training.

Three days later the gang struck again. They stole a van and a taxi as getaway cars and hit two jewellery shops in west Kowloon. The gang all wore balaclavas and had AK-47s slung over their shoulders. They were considerably better equipped than the police and it took them less than four minutes to snatch HK$8.7 million worth of gold ornaments. This time they grabbed a woman hostage. They fired at the police as they fled and, ruthless to the end, even sprayed an ambulance with bullets as it sped towards the scene. The gang drove for ten minutes, then dumped the hostage and switched from the taxi to the van. Yet again they escaped with their booty. No one was killed, but a number of officers sustained cuts on their arms and faces from shattered windscreens.

Police spent the next six months tracking down Yip Kai-foon. They found out where he was hiding by tracing telephone calls to him. He was living in Yuen Long, in the north-west New Territories. Early one morning, the police surrounded the house, smashed down the front door, and barged inside. With guns raised, they ran through the house ready to confront the notorious gangster, but the house was empty. Had they called before they burst in, they would have discovered that the telephone rang in a different house. Yip had his telephone calls forwarded to another residence, three doors down, and had run when he heard the police.

Knowing that the law was on his tail, Yip Kai-foon fled to the Mainland, where he lived under the protection of a relative who was an important government official. He spent most of his time in Shanwei, occasionally popping in to see his parents at the family home.

On the Mainland Yip Kai-foon was free to do as he wanted and was often spotted in the city's karaoke bars. Here in Shanwei, Yip was known as a tough, hotshot gangster, but in Hong Kong he had an even more impressive title—he was the territory's most wanted man. There was a HK$500,000 bounty on his head, a reward that was later increased to HK$1 million.

The police knew of his whereabouts, but there was little they could do to catch him on the Mainland. One police officer revealed: 'We knew where he was, which village, which street, even the house number. But we couldn't get him because he was protected by the PLA [People's Liberation Army], and the PSB [Public Security Bureau] couldn't get in.'

By late 1994, Yip had spent much of the booty from the Hong Kong robberies and needed more cash. Increasing affluence in southern China meant that there were many places to hit in Guangdong without even having to cross the border to Hong Kong. During 1995, Yip and his gang launched a series of robberies in Shenzhen and Guangzhou. As Yip Kai-foon became famous, he also became more ruthless. He knew he was treading a thin line and, without the luxury of anonymity, had to keep a constant eye on his back. By the end of the year he knew he was being trailed and, determined to put an end to it, he made a public display of his anger. On 27 November he shot dead a police informant on the street in Shenzhen. The killing was in broad daylight, a warning that 'grasses' (informers) would not be tolerated.

If informants knew how to track down Yip Kai-foon, Cheung certainly did too. After his release from prison in 1995, he got in touch with Yip and shared his big plan. It would take months of surveillance and organization, but that was Cheung's forte. Cheung wanted to hold a tycoon for ransom and he went straight for the jackpot, Li Ka-shing, Hong Kong's most prominent businessman. The billionaire is revered as a god in Hong Kong and is living proof that even a refugee can become outrageously rich. Li began by sweeping the floor in a plastics factory and through hard work and wise investments became a property giant. Yet despite his wealth, he never forgot where he came from. Like Yip, Li was Chao Zhou and his home town remained important to him: he helped develop power in the area and built Shantou University.

The kidnapping would never have been more than a pipe dream for most of Guangzhou's petty criminals, but Cheung could make it happen. He did not plan to kidnap the seventy-one-year-old Li, but his eldest son, Victor. He spent months doing his homework, tracking the tycoon, and organizing the weapons—sources said that he gave Yip Kai-foon HK$1.4 million to buy guns. So it was that on 13 May 1996 that Yip and his gang of five slipped into Hong Kong on a speedboat. It was no ordinary speedboat, but a *dai fei*, an illegally modified craft with five engines. At the time *dai fei* were the fastest boats on the South China Sea and could easily outrun police launches. They turned off their lights and pulled up to the harbour wall in Kennedy Town, west of Central. It was 4.30am and pitch black. They leapt from the *dai fei* onto the steps of a small landing.

The gang hurried down a narrow alley that runs from the jetty to the main road. They paused at the end of the alley to get their bearings, but their timing could not have been worse. Two police officers, on their routine beat along the waterfront, spotted the disorientated group and immediately suspected them to be illegal immigrants. The policemen shouted for them to stop, and then the silence was broken by the sound of pistols being cocked. As the officers went for their guns, the group fled down the road, except for one man. Yip told the gang to run—he would take care of this.

'Stop or we'll shoot,' one of the officers demanded. The police saw Yip's silhouette turn and point a gun at them. One of the officers took aim and fired. He had been on the force for twelve years, but it was the first time he had fired a gun on duty. Yip took the shot and ran. The second shot appeared to slow him down and he turned and levelled his Black Star automatic pistol at the police. The officer fired again and Yip slumped to the ground. The gangster was down, but he was not about to give up and, holding his gun with both hands, he raised it. The constables dived behind the gates of a bus depot and a second later heard the shrill sound of a bullet as it ricocheted off the gate.

A third policeman had heard the gunfire and rushed to the scene, taking cover behind a low wall. He ordered Yip to drop his gun, but Yip raised his pistol and pulled the trigger. Nothing happened; his gun had jammed. The constable fired and Yip slumped to the ground, a dark pool of blood spreading around his body. A blue travel bag lay abandoned on the street. Inside the police found 1.8 kg of Chinese army explosives—enough to kill anyone within a 200-metre radius—a Russian 7.62mm automatic machine gun loaded with twelve rounds of ammunition, and two radio-controlled switching devices.

Yip was carrying an ID card in the name of Lau Chi-cheung, but it was not until he was admitted to Queen Mary Hospital and routinely

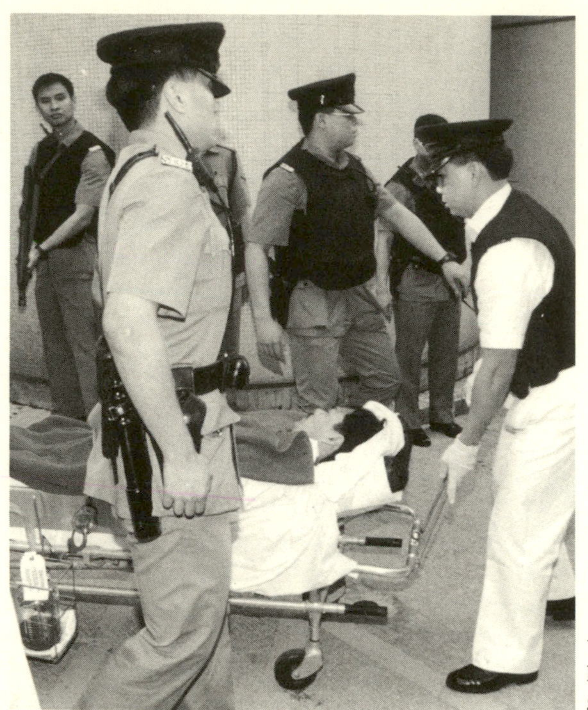

Yip Kai-foon is taken to hospital after losing a gun battle with police

fingerprinted that police realized who they had caught. He looked very different from the mugshot taken when he had first been arrested twelve years earlier. He had changed his hairstyle, grown a moustache, and even had a mole on the left side of his chin removed. But there were also changes beyond the obvious attempts at disguise: his face was leaner and his cheekbones more prominent, but the most startling change was in his eyes. In his youth, his eyes had been fairly large, but over the years they had narrowed. Now they were dark slits, as though he were squinting into the sun.

The realization that Yip Kai-foon had been caught was greeted with a mixture of euphoria and panic. The police could not believe their luck. After years of plotting to catch Hong Kong's most wanted criminal , it was a stroke of luck that led them to Yip. He had been hit three times: one bullet had pierced his waist, another his arm, and the third had smashed his spine, leaving him paralysed from the waist down. Although there was no chance of Yip escaping unaided, police feared a counterattack and stationed armed officers in bullet-proof vests to patrol the hospital's corridors and staircases. Despite the high security, both staff and patients were terrified; Yip was known as a man of violence and he had already escaped from this hospital once before. After just one day, police could not control the rising panic in the hospital due to Yip's presence, nor could they guarantee the safety of those inside, and Yip was transferred to Stanley Prison. It was a strange sight. Hong Kong's most wanted man, now crippled, left hospital on a stretcher, surrounded by dozens of armed guards.

Yip's arrest upset Cheung's plan, but didn't sabotage it. Ten days after Yip was shot, Cheung and a gang of nine men abducted Victor Li as he was being driven from his house on the south side of Hong Kong Island to Central on the north side. Masked and armed with AK-47s and pistols, they surrounded his car and fired a warning shot through the window. Li was bound and blindfolded and driven to Sheung Shui, a town bordering the Mainland. He was taken to a small hut and forced to strip to his underwear. Then the kidnappers called Li's wife and demanded a staggering HK$1 billion ransom.

Cheung stayed in the hut with Victor Li. According to a mainland newspaper, Cheung shared his philosophy of life with Li while waiting for the ransom: 'My creed is that I cannot allow myself to be poor. I don't have the time or the patience to make a living by doing proper jobs. I can't work as hard as other people. Life is very short and fragile. I'm already more than forty. If I want to get rich I must take some unconventional steps. Money is the most important thing in the world, without which you cannot do anything. But it's only me who can kidnap tycoons. No one else can do such things.'

Cheung must have been impressed when the ransom demand was met the following day, in cash. Victor Li was immediately released. He never reported the kidnapping to the police and, years later, he has never acknowledged that it took place. Despite his silence, Li displayed the telltale signs of someone who had had a brush with the rougher side of life, and from then on there were few places he went without his bodyguards. Pleased with how smoothly the kidnapping had gone, Cheung began plotting a second abduction. Again he chose a top Hong Kong tycoon, this time the chairman of Sun Hung Kai Properties, Walter Kwok Ping-sheung.

Meanwhile, Yip was confined to a wheelchair in Stanley Prison. He was charged over the stash of explosives and weapons, but was not giving away any clues about Cheung and the gang. When pressed for information about their whereabouts, Yip merely issued a series of complaints: he could not see the television from his cell, he was beaten by prison officers, and he demanded the barrister of his choice, Kevin Egan. He even went on hunger strike, but this was not taken seriously as his brother supplied him with biscuits throughout his fast. He insisted on his right to weekly bail hearings, which were costly because of the high security. Two hundred police were posted outside the court, a helicopter flew overhead, and everyone who entered the court was searched. At his first hearing in July, he was handed the additional charges of escaping from custody and kidnapping two people, the man he had forced to drive to Aberdeen and the man's son.

By September, Cheung was set for his second kidnapping. The strategy was much the same as before: Walter Kwok was snatched while being driven home and taken to the hut in Sheung Shui. There he was stripped to his underpants, blindfolded, and his hands tied. In addition, there was a further humiliation; he was forced into a small wooden box that had only a few holes in it for ventilation. Kwok was

Barrister Kevin Egan

only allowed out of the trunk to go to the toilet and to eat a daily meal of roast pork. Since Kwok was not as wealthy as Victor Li, Cheung dropped his ransom demand, but it was still a hefty HK$600 million. Kwok spent six days in his claustrophobic cell before his family came up with the ransom. Like Li, he never reported his kidnapping.

Cheung pocketed about half of the ransom money from the kidnappings: HK$738 million. As Yip was in prison, his HK$75 million cut was given to his elder brother. Yip is unlikely to see that money for a long time, if ever. On 10 March 1997, he was jailed for forty-one years. His earliest release date is 2022, when he will be sixty. While Yip will have to wait to spend his money, Cheung wasted no time. Sources said he laundered much of the money by buying luxury cars, as well as fifty flats in Guangdong. He also spent a lot on his favourite pastime, gambling, and lost HK$300 million.

There were rumours in the press that a large-scale manhunt for Cheung was mounted in the Mainland following a personal complaint by Li Ka-shing to President Jiang Zemin. This is despite the fact that Li refused to report the kidnapping to the Hong Kong police. If this rumour is correct, it suggests that Li has little faith in the Hong Kong authorities.

In December 1997, Hong Kong police tracked Cheung down to another Sheung Shui village hut. Worried about alerting him, the police carried out round-the-clock surveillance for weeks, secretly filming Cheung and his men as they went back and forth between Hong Kong and the Mainland. Police suspected that Cheung was hiding drugs, but when they took soil samples from around the hut they began to realize what was going on. Analysis of the soil samples revealed the presence of explosives. The next time Cheung went away, police decided to search the hut, even though it risked alerting him to the surveillance. They found a huge stash of explosives, 818 kg, enough to blow up a building. The find made front-page news and Cheung immediately fled to the Mainland.

Cheung had allegedly ordered the explosives from a contact in the casino of the Lisboa Hotel in Macau and they had been smuggled from mainland China to the hut. There were popular theories about what Cheung planned to do with that amount of explosives. One police source insists he was going to 'wage a campaign of terrorism on Hong Kong'. Another theory holds that he planned to carry out a personal vendetta by bombing Stanley Prison and perhaps even trying to free Yip.

After an eleven-day search, Cheung was caught on 28 January 1998, and held at a rural detention centre in Guangdong. But he was not about to make life easy for the authorities—even confirmation of his identity took hours. Only when the names of his family were read out did he admit he was Cheung Tze-keung. But he was not about to be broken down easily, nor did he let his guard slip. When asked to sign the interrogation notes, he carefully checked the statement before signing and drew seventy lines in the empty space of the last page to make sure nothing else could be added.

The breakthrough for mainland authorities came in April 1998 when a Hong Kong suspect, Cheung Chi-fung, hoping to get a lighter sentence, revealed the name of another gangster. He also said he had witnessed Yip Kai-foon kill the police informant in Shenzhen. During a raid on Yip's family home in Shanwei, Guangdong police found HK$13.75 million hidden under the kitchen floor. In July of that year, the Guangdong Security Bureau announced the arrest of fourteen more people, including Yip's brothers. The gang were charged with a range of offences committed over the previous eight years, from murder, kidnapping, and robbery to extortion and the smuggling of explosives.

Cheung's appeal was denied and he was executed on 5 December 1998. The arrest of Cheung and his gang raised questions about the way mainland authorities press their charges. The two kidnappings in Hong Kong were punishable on the Mainland because they were planned there. Although the victims were never taken to the Mainland, according to section six of the Chinese criminal code, a crime is deemed to have occurred on Chinese territory (the Mainland) if it or its results take place there. Cheung and his gang were prosecuted based on their confessions, a legally questionable practice according to Hong Kong law.

The situation is unusual and casts doubt on the Mainland's legal procedures, as Victor Li and Walter Kwok never reported the kidnappings and were not prepared to give evidence in court. Thus, a crime that has gone unreported in Hong Kong may be punishable on the Mainland. What is there to stop the wealthy and influential from using their power to bypass the local authorities to obtain justice through the Mainland's judicial systems? And what is there to stop Mainland police from punishing a Hong Kong person by extracting a confession from him that he orchestrated a murder, or other crime, even if the victim is faceless?

Cheung Tze-keung's case gave a number of Hong Kong people pause for thought, not least because the Mainland's legal and judicial systems give a much lower priority to the protection of the rights of defendants.

The myth about Cheung became larger than the man himself. It was reported that it took two bullets to execute him; this may have been the case, or it may have signalled the beginning of the legend of a man who had the audacity to carry off some of Hong Kong's most outrageous crimes. Forty-three when he died, Cheung was still young enough to become a cult figure. The same cannot be said of Yip Kai-foon, who is rotting away in his wheelchair in prison. Paralysed and pathetic, Yip has all but given up on life.

Broken Tooth: Macau's Casino Wars

The New Century Hotel on Taipa Island, south of the Macau peninsula, faces the sea. Like many of the enclave's plush hotels, the building is swathed in neon and trimmed with fairy lights. On 30 July 1997, the hotel was empty aside from a few resident guests. It was a few hours after midnight and two Portuguese security guards were busy installing extra surveillance cameras outside the hotel. The men were brothers and Jose Rodrigues, at twenty-eight, was the elder of the two. He had been working for Guardforce for three years and was no stranger to violence, but even he was thrown by what happened that night.

Halfway through the job they were having a cigarette break when their idle banter was broken by the screech of tyres. A car sped around the corner and even before it pulled up in front of the hotel, two masked men leaned out of the rear windows firing M-16 assault rifles. Jose was hit in the leg and dived behind a car for cover. Over the thunder of gunfire he heard his brother, Nuno, scream. Jose peered from behind the car and saw his brother doubled over.

'Get down,' Jose shouted, and he stumbled towards Nuno. A volley of bullets chased him and he dropped to the pavement. Throwing an arm protectively over his brother, he tucked his head down as the shrapnel spat in his face. The other gunman fired relentlessly at the hotel, smashing its glass facade. He whipped up his rifle, spraying an arc of bullets in the air and shattering the second-floor windows.

The attack lasted only a few minutes and the gunmen sped off, crashing through the arm of an automatic parking barrier. They fired

Wan Kuok-koi

at a car as they raced across the bridge to the Macau peninsula, presumably fearing that it was the police. But it wasn't. Although Jose had called for help immediately, it was twenty minutes before the police arrived.

There was more violence that night. An hour after the attack a home-made fire bomb built from firecracker gunpowder was thrown into the Governor's Palace. Jose had known there was a good chance of trouble that night, but he hadn't expected to be a target. He was lucky to escape alive; so far that year sixteen people had been killed in a bitter triad turf war. The usually tranquil Portuguese-run enclave had been thrown into chaos by two gangs fighting over the most lucrative sector of the gambling industry, the private VIP gaming rooms. In November 1996, the head of Macau's Gambling Inspectorate, Lieutenant Colonel Manuel Antonio Apolinario, was shot twice by a hit man on the back of a motorbike. The bullets passed through his cheek and neck, but he survived. The style of attack was repeated many times over the next two years. Motorbikes are the easiest way of navigating Macau's narrow lanes and making a quick escape. Rumour had it that the hit men were hired assassins from the Mainland who were paid a set fee for every corpse left in their wake.

As the struggle for control of the VIP rooms heated up, so the casualties mounted. Everyone involved in the gambling industry was a potential victim. In April 1997, a Hong Kong businessman who organized gambling jaunts to Macau for 'high rollers' was shot three times in the stomach but survived. Those whose job it was to keep an eye on the casinos and control the violence were obvious targets, as were their families. The relative of a policeman was killed following the officer's investigations. Locals became wary about going out at night and tourists had second thoughts about visiting.

The violence came to a head on 4 May 1997, when three 14K mobsters were attacked. A hit man, riding on the back of a motorcycle, drew up alongside their car on a busy main road and fired nine shots through the window. The triads took three bullets each and none survived. One of the victims was allegedly the right-hand man of the 14K's chief, or 'dragonhead'. The murders would not be brushed off lightly and leaders of the rival gang, the Wo On Lok, met heads of the 14K to try to negotiate a tentative peace. The violence had given Macau bad international press, scaring off thousands of would-be visitors and gamblers and putting a big dent in the tourist dollar. It was an acknowledgment of the damage to business that drew the rival gangs together for talks. Their discussions achieved a lull in the violence, but the calm was short-lived. There was trouble brewing within the ranks of the 14K and a leadership struggle saw Wan Kuok-koi—better known as Broken Tooth—and Ng Wai wrapped in a vicious duel. The struggle was made all the more bitter because they had once been partners and friends. Ng Wai was nicknamed 'Kai Sze' ('market') Wai because he used to run the protection rackets in Hong Kong's Mong Kok market. In the early 1980s, he left Hong Kong and moved to the Philippines. There, with the help of former President Ferdinand Marcos, he became involved with casinos and received his education in the gambling industry. He also met the woman who would become his wife. She was streetwise and savvy, but more importantly she had influential contacts in the gambling underworld. It was with the help of her connections that they moved to Macau in 1987 and Kai Sze Wai negotiated a generous portion of the 14K's VIP rooms. But his success had to do with timing, and the help of Broken Tooth. When Kai Sze Wai arrived on the scene, Broken Tooth saw him as the perfect ally to help oust another 14K mobster, Ping Mo-Ding, who was getting too big for his boots and had made many enemies. Broken Tooth succeeded in kicking Ping out of the casinos and ultimately out of Macau.

For years Broken Tooth and Kai Sze Wai worked alongside each other, managing their VIP rooms and raking in millions each month from the high rollers' tables. But the balance of power shifted as Broken Tooth became stronger. His rise to the top was not easy, but he was a tough street fighter and his fearlessness won him much respect. His forearms were criss-crossed with scars, a legacy of his bravado, and he had lost nine teeth. Although he had his teeth replaced with false ones, he retained his nickname, Broken Tooth. In an exclusive interview with *Time* magazine, Wan said that Kai Sze Wai was envious of his position and had offered the rival Wo On Lok triads a bigger cut of the VIP gaming rooms if they killed Wan. It was this death threat, Broken Tooth claimed, that sparked the war between the two gangs in late 1996.

By surviving the attempts on his life, Broken Tooth became even stronger and gained more followers. From his new position of power he succeeded in ousting Kai Sze Wai from the casino in the Lisboa Hotel, Macau's most prestigious gambling spot. In his rival's place he opened his own private rooms, the Wan Hao Club.

Forced to give up his lucrative VIP rooms, Kai Sze Wai took over the 600-room New Century Hotel and prepared to open his own twenty-four-hour casino there. It would be Macau's tenth casino. Taipa Island had been of little interest to the triads until 1995. That was the year that Macau opened its first airport, bringing with it hotels and casinos. But Broken Tooth had not ousted Kai Sze Wai from the Lisboa only to see him set up nearby. He saw himself as the king of the triads and began a campaign to terrorize his rival. First he issued a warning that anyone who went to Kai Sze Wai's VIP rooms would make themselves his enemy. Then he had posters printed and distributed throughout Macau claiming that Kai Sze Wai was a drug dealer. His next step was to show Kai Sze Wai that he was out for blood.

Knowing these were not idle threats, Kai Sze Wai dared not leave his hotel. For the whole of July 1997 the New Century was his hideaway. He lived and dined like a king, but he was trapped. He was a pathetic creature, forced to turn his own home into a prison. On 30 July, three days before the casino was due to open, he received two threatening phone calls from Broken Tooth. He took on extra security and was scrupulous in checking the men who protected him. Fearing that Chinese hit men might infiltrate his hotel-fortress, he employed only foreign security guards. That was why Jose Rodriguez and his brother were installing extra surveillance cameras in the early hours of the morning.

The day after the attack, the brothers were in hospital. Both had been shot in the leg. The bullet that hit Jose had blasted a tunnel clean through his thigh, but the one that hit Nuno was still lodged in his leg. Nuno was in surgery having it removed when Jose's mobile rang. The phone's digital display showed that the call came from China.

Without identifying himself, the caller said: 'How are you? How is your brother?' Jose said that they were recovering and would be okay. 'That wasn't supposed to happen,' the caller said and he rung off without waiting for a response.

Jose was sure that the speaker was Broken Tooth, but it wasn't until weeks later that his suspicions were confirmed. He was with friends in a night-club when he spotted the gangster. He was not surprised to see Broken Tooth out because he knew the triad was a big fan of dance music and liked to party. Jose kept an eye on Broken Tooth and followed when he saw him walk towards the men's room. The toilet was one of the few places he could get the notorious gangster alone, and even then there would doubtless be a bodyguard close by. Broken Tooth rarely went anywhere alone—he had too many enemies.

Broken Tooth was standing in front of the wash basin when Jose walked in. The gangster looked at Jose in the mirror, his face showing no flicker of surprise, as though he were expecting him. 'That wasn't meant to happen,' the triad said simply, then he walked out.

It was an apology—Broken Tooth's men rarely made mistakes. The Secretary for Security, Manuel Monge, made this point when he tried to comfort the public and boost the flagging tourist industry. 'Do not worry,' he said reassuringly, 'These men are professionals, they do not miss.' But tourists were not encouraged by the admission that Macau's killers were top-class assassins, and Brigadier Monge soon found himself one step closer to the violence. His driver would be added to the list of victims, but not before a series of attacks on gambling inspectors.

Jose Madeira, a twenty-six-year-old gambling inspector, had been in his job only two months when he was shot in the face with a sawn-off shotgun. He survived the attack outside the Macau Palace Floating Restaurant casino, but was left with horrific facial injuries. The campaign of intimidation was stepped up the following month when the homes of three gambling inspectors were firebombed. The bombs were crude petrol ones, easy to make and launch, but capable of causing panic. They were a classic triad terror device.

It was in this climate of fear that Brigadier Monge's driver was sent a gift-wrapped snake. The serpent's tail had been sliced in two, a traditional triad death threat. A few days later the driver was shot dead. Later that month, gambling inspector Francisco Amaral was assassinated. The twenty-six-year-old had only had the job for four months and was walking to lunch with a friend when he was shot at point-blank range. The government described his murder as the 'perfect execution'. It underlined the fact that something had to be done urgently about the triad violence. Gangland slayings had claimed the lives of twenty people so far that year.

The Macau Legislative Assembly took the biggest step towards halting the anarchy by introducing new anti-triad laws replacing a 1978 bill. Under the old bill, it was legal to be a triad. But now gang membership was outlawed and spelt a minimum three-year jail term. Senior triads could be handed a hefty twelve-year sentence. The change gave the police new powers, making it easier for them to arrest gangsters. The legislation brought with it a witness protection scheme to encourage triads to give evidence against their bosses.

Broken Tooth was among the first to be charged under the new anti-triad law, but he avoided the warrant for his arrest by leaving Macau for a while. When he returned, a Portuguese judge cancelled the warrant and dropped the charges against him. It was an unprecedented move, but there was no time for an explanation because the next day the judge took early retirement and returned to Portugal. Another warrant was issued for his arrest, this one by the mainland police in neighbouring Zhuhai, but it soon became obvious that palms were being greased. The Chinese judge was found guilty of corruption and the warrant was dropped. It looked as though Broken Tooth had Kai Sze Wai to thank for the warrants.

Triad violence could not be exorcised with the wave of a legislative wand. On 1 May 1998, the car of Judiciary Director Dr Antonio Marques Baptista was bombed. He heard the explosion during his morning jog; it was a narrow escape. The Judiciary Director was determined to punish this outrage. Within hours, the Lisboa Hotel was surrounded by dozens of officers in bullet-proof vests, and Broken Tooth was arrested in one of the hotel's restaurants. Nineteen months later, his case remained in limbo thanks to a combination of fear of retribution and inefficiency.

A major setback occurred when the judge presiding over the trial resigned, ostensibly for health reasons. It was widely assumed that he quit fearing for his life and the safety of his family. Several months passed before another judge could be brought in from Portugal. Then followed an epidemic of 'witness amnesia'; many people simply kept silent in the face of a man who wielded so much power. It may not have been coincidence that the director of the prison where Broken Tooth was incarcerated resigned soon after his most notorious prisoner arrived. Other security staff quit when they were called on to testify. Even from behind bars the gangster could make people jump. The evidence against him is largely police intelligence and much of the pending case depends on how much credence is given to the testimonies of unnamed officers.

As if Broken Tooth's arrest did not garner enough attention, six days after his arrest a movie based on his life and financed by the triad himself screened in Hong Kong. *Casino* was due to open in Macau the following day, but was banned. On 6 May 1998, presumably in retaliation against the ban, more than fifty cars were set alight within two hours in Macau. The bombs were crude devices, little more than paper being set alight and shoved in the gas tank of a car or the exhaust pipe of a motorbike. The film itself was more violent and the authenticity of many of the fighting scenes can be put down to the fact that some of the actors were triads. Although the script was apparently carefully written to get as close as possible to the real story without the fear of litigation, Broken Tooth couldn't resist leaving a few clues for anti-triad investigators. For example, many of the characters' names are homophones of those of real characters. And ironically, Broken Tooth was played by Simon Yam, the brother of a Hong Kong anti-triad officer. During filming Yam was serving a three-year ban from casinos for breaching an exclusion order.

On 23 November 1999 Wan was convicted of being a triad member and leader as well as of money laundering, loan-sharking, and telephone tapping. He received the maximum sentence of fifteen years.